D1283110

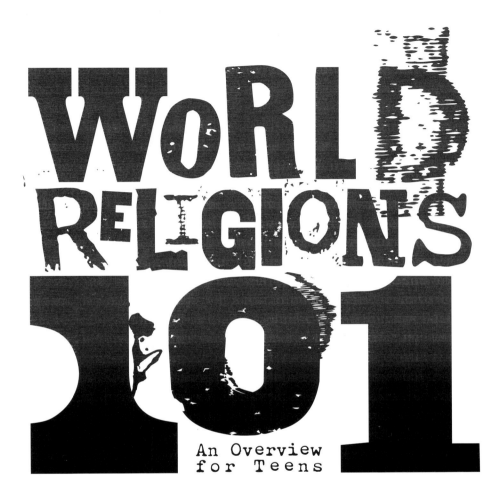

An Overview
for Teens

WORLD RELIGIONS 101

An Overview for Teens

Margaret O. Hyde & Emily G. Hyde

TF
CB

Twenty-First Century Books

Minneapolis

The images in this book are used with the permission of: © Chuck Nacke/Time Life Pictures/Getty Images, p. 11; © Katja Heinemann/Aurora/Getty Images, p. 13; © Image Asset Management Ltd./SuperStock, p. 22 (both); © Sherab/Alamy, p. 28; © Visual Arts Library (London)/Alamy, p. 33; © DAJ/Getty Images, p. 37; © Bridgeman Art Library, London/SuperStock, p. 38; © Foto Marburg/Art Resource, NY, p. 41; © NARINDER NANU/AFP/Getty Images, p. 43; © Jim West/ZUMA Press, p. 49; © Fred Mayer/Hulton Archive/Getty Images, p. 55; © ORLANDO SIERRA/AFP/Getty Images, p. 64; © Paula Bronstein/Getty Images, p. 66; AP Photo/Hasan Sarbakhshian, p. 68; © Sean Gallup/Getty Images, p. 73; © ArkReligion.com/Alamy, p. 80; AP Photo, p. 83; Library of Congress (LC-USZ61-215), p. 87; © James P. Blair/National Geographic/Getty Images, p. 89; © NGUYEN PHUONG THAO/AFP/Getty Images, p. 91; © Alan Levenson/Stone/Getty Images, p. 95; © Nucleus Medical Art/Visuals Unlimited, p. 99; AP Photo/Kathy Willens, p. 100; Dr Michael Persinger and Stanley Koren (Laurentian University). Photo by Paul Valliant, p. 110.

Text copyright © 2009 by Margaret O. Hyde and Emily G. Hyde

Twenty-First Century Books
A division of Lerner Publishing Group, Inc.
241 First Avenue North
Minneapolis, Minnesota 55401 U.S.A.

Website address: www.lernerbooks.com

Library of Congress Cataloging in Publication Data

Hyde, Margaret O. (Margaret Oldroyd)
    World religions 101 : an overview for teens / by Margaret O. Hyde and Emily
  G. Hyde.
        p.   cm. — (Teen overviews)
    Includes bibliographical references and index.
    ISBN 978–0–8225–7518–4 (lib. bdg. : alk. paper)
    1. Teenagers—Religious life. 2. Spirituality. 3. Spiritual life. 4. Religions.
  I. Hyde, Emily G. II. Title. III. Title: World religions one hundred and one.
  IV. Title: World religions one hundred one.
  BL625.47.H93 2009
  204—dc22   2007049492

Manufactured in the United States of America
1 2 3 4 5 6 – BP – 14 13 12 11 10 09

CONTENTS

CHAPTER 1

SPIRITUALITY AND RELIGION

Marta feels spiritual whenever she walks in the woods. She took a course in astronomy that made her feel the same way. Steven's feelings of spirituality are different from Marta's. He is aware of being spiritual only when kneeling at prayer or sitting in his church. He likes organized religion for its established set of beliefs.

People around the world search for spiritual meaning in their lives in many different ways. Spirituality is one of the ways you find meaning, hope, comfort, and inner peace in your life. Spirituality is personal, and everyone's path is unique. You may find it in music, nature, or art. Many people increase their feelings of spirituality when they meditate, pray, sing, read, volunteer, or do yoga or tai chi. Anything that gives a sense of connection, love, and strength can increase spirituality. It is looking inward, searching for meaning and purpose, and seeking to understand what really matters. The most common path to spirituality around the world is through religion.

Who Is Spiritual?

Even if you have never entered a church, synagogue, mosque, or other place of religious worship, you might be spiritual. You may be an atheist, one who believes there is no god or gods, and you may still be spiritual.

Spirituality is all around you. You may be reading a book about spiritual guidelines for lasting relationships in love, or you may be watching a Muslim program on your iPod. You might find a website with a message to Skye, a girl who was killed in a car crash last week. The message reads: "Hey Skye, We miss you but we know you must be enjoying heaven. Rest in peace, but don't forget us. From Your Friends, (Signed) Mat and Asia." You may have a spiritual experience when you are alone at the edge of a lake watching a sunset, or you may feel close to God, or Allah, at the birth of a baby. You may find spiritual fulfillment in exploring the cosmos, art, nature, your breathing, and even yourself.

The word *spirituality* comes from the Latin *spiritus,* which means "breath," as in the breath of life. Spirituality is generally considered an awareness of yourself and a sense of connection to nature, a higher being, or to some purpose other than yourself. Spirituality is broader than religion, which is a specific system of attitudes, beliefs, and practices. Still, all organized religions have a strong spiritual aspect.

While spiritual life has been called the heart of all religions, increasing numbers of people call themselves spiritual rather than religious. Attendance at many old, established religious places of worship is decreasing, both in Europe and the United States, while spiritual movements seem to be exploding. References to spirituality on the Internet have mushroomed since the year 2000, with the number running in the millions.

Many scholars who study religion believe we are living in a time of spiritual revolution, a period when religion is giving way to spirituality worldwide. Whether people believe in God or not, most people have a sense of the spiritual. As seekers search for passion and depth in their lives, they ask: Who am I? Why am I here? Where am I going? What will happen when I die?

Humans Are Spiritual Beings

Artifacts from prehistoric people who lived one hundred thousand years ago show that humans have long expressed an awareness of spirit and an inner self. Excavated burial sites have revealed that these people buried their dead with tools and weapons, perhaps as something they could use in an afterlife or as an offering to their gods. In caves in France, where the oldest known paintings in the world have been found, certain figures are believed to be signs of spiritual activity. These paintings were probably created thirty thousand years ago.

In the animist beliefs of many traditional indigenous (native) peoples around the world, all living things are believed to have spirits. As long as ten thousand years ago, when Siberia, Russia, and Alaska were still connected by a land bridge, men and women called shamans were believed to speak to spirits and receive their messages. If you were a member of an ancient tribal society and you had a health problem, bad luck, or needed another kind of help, you would probably consult your local shaman. He or she would go into a trance by singing, fasting (eating no food), drumming, or another method to consult the spirit world. In animist faith systems, all natural beings, objects, and events share spirit, or consciousness. Therefore, the spirits of ancestors can communicate with the living.

Shamanism is sometimes called the first religion, although it was never systematically organized. A shaman in one part of the world knew nothing about the shamans in other parts. Shamans play a role in the spiritual lives of people in many parts of the modern world too. In modern times, New Age Shamanism is a free-flowing movement that exists without central organization.

An interest in spirituality is a core part of human life. Spirituality includes a capacity for creativity, growth, and the development of a value system. Religion is just one expression of spirituality but by far the most common one.

In his book *The Varieties of Religious Experience* (1902), William James, a famous American psychologist and philosopher, says that religion "consists of the belief that there is an unseen order, and that our supreme good lies in harmoniously adjusting ourselves thereto."

Religion, then, usually involves believing in and seeking to live in harmony with an underlying reality.

Throughout the world, people give purpose and meaning to their lives through religious practice and other forms of spirituality. No matter where they live, worshippers seek something greater than the here and now. In a November 2007 Harris Poll reported by the Reuters news service, 75 percent of adult Americans believed in heaven.

Teens and Religion

Most U.S. teens who attend religious services do so in Christian churches, Jewish synagogues, or Islamic mosques. Many other young people are drawn to ecospirituality—a spiritual view of people's relation-ship with the universe. These young people find spirituality through the wonders of nature. Modern young people may seem less religious to their elders,

Muslim teens stand outside a mosque in California.

but many young people are religious in different ways than in the past.

Wendy is a teen who spent some time in South Korea as part of a student exchange program. In South Korea, she visited a group of Buddhists who worshipped silently at their home in a monastery. She began practicing some of their prayers every morning. When Wendy returned to the United States, she continued to spend a short time in silent prayer each morning. Wendy did not join a church, but she believes her prayers help her cope with problems in her life.

From the monastery to the superchurch, religious experience widely varies for teens as a way to express spirituality. It ranges from a girl who worships at a small Buddhist shrine in her home to a large group of Muslims gathering in a mosque. In France, a 2007 law removed a ban on Muslim women wearing head scarves in their college classes as a sign of their Islamic faith. In that country, Muslim girls are discussing the issue of the right to public religious expression. Far away, young Hindus are preparing the body of a man for cremation on the banks of the Ganges, a sacred river in India. While a group of Tibetan monks are meditating in an American monastery in complete silence, a group of American teens celebrate their religion with singing and rock music. This vibrant group of young Christians is called the disciple generation, after the disciples, or first followers, of Jesus.

The Disciple Generation

Every song at the rock concert was about Jesus. The thousand-member audience was on its feet, waving

Teens attend a Christian rock festival in Pennsylvania.

hands stretched toward the ceiling, electrified by the words and the music. They were high on Christ.

These people belong to what has been called the disciple generation, the rising American counterculture that accepts Jesus as a personal savior and shares an intense faith that unites believers against what they feel is the spiritual emptiness of the world. They believe every word in the Bible is true, and they are spreading the word about it everywhere they go. They are part of a growing Evangelical movement with tens of thousands of U.S. members. They are spreading a message of the love of Christ and of traditional social values.

Many teens are drawn to this Evangelical form of Christianity. Evangelical Christians believe in a literal understanding of the Bible and consider themselves to be born again when they accept Jesus as their personal savior in their religious lives. Many teens learn about the Evangelical message at skateboard festivals, rock concerts, coffeehouses, warehouses, homes, open fields, barns, and other places where Evangelical events are held. The spiritual message—"Jesus loves you"—is simple and appealing. In fact, many teens tattoo this message on their bodies.

Author Lauren Sandler describes the growing Evangelical youth subculture in her book *Righteous: Dispatches from the Evangelical Youth Movement* (2006). This Evangelical movement is very different from youth groups in formal churches where participants worship in ways similar to the way their parents do—reading the Bible, listening to a teacher, and singing the same hymns that their grandparents sang. For the disciple generation, expressing Christ's love is a practice that takes place beyond the limits of the church itself, in rock concerts and other public venues, and involves less established methods of worship.

Organized Religion

Spiritual seekers around the world search for meaning and purpose in their lives in an endless number of ways as they foster the capacity to experience awe, gratitude, reverence, love, and peace. Spirituality covers a wide range of experiences and emotions.

Most world religions include the belief in one or more deities (gods and goddesses), a doctrine (set of teachings), rituals, stories, ceremonies, and a code of conduct. The ten most common religions in the world, according to size, are Christianity, Islam, Hinduism,

KABBALAH

Many young people of all faiths have discovered the quiet wisdom and have experienced the powerful effects of studying a modern version of Kabbalah. Kabbalah is the world's oldest surviving body of written spiritual wisdom. Modern Kabbalah has its roots in Judaism. In modern popular culture, however, Kabbalah is a way of life that is meant to enhance many different religious practices. Many celebrities of various religions are involved in the Kabbalah movement worldwide.

Kabbalah teaches that every human being is a work in progress. It is based on studies that intend to free individuals from the domination of the human ego to create affinity with the sharing essence of God. The studies give people tools for positive change.

Many young people, from Jerusalem to Los Angeles, are wearing red string Kabbalah bracelets to ward off evil. They believe the bracelets protect them from the influences of the evil eye, a powerful negative force that, in ancient times, was thought to cause havoc. In modern times, the evil eye may be experienced in many ways, such as through unkind glances from people around them.

Buddhism, Sikhism, Judaism, Bahaism, Confucianism, Jainism, and Shintoism.

In the United States, if you were born to Christian parents, chances are good that you would become a Christian. Or if you were born to Jewish parents, you would grow up as a Jew. If you were born in India, you would probably be a Hindu or possibly a Sikh. If you were born in Iran, you are mostly likely to be a Muslim. In Japan you might be Buddhist or Shinto; or in

China, Buddhist or Taoist. However, many Americans are switching faiths or dropping out of formal religious practice altogether. In the United States, 25 percent of adults leave the faith of their upbringing, according to a survey released in February 2008 by the Pew Forum on Religion and Public Life. Many nondenominational churches—those not associated with a particular religion—are gaining members.

Religious seekers come in thousands of varieties. Their groups range in size from single individuals to groups that number in the millions. Even the size of congregations that participate in worship services of the same religion varies widely. For example, Christians range from those who worship on their own, to small groups who attend house churches where people meet in homes, to members of megachurches where thousands gather. Many of the Americans who do not go to church, temple, or mosque seek spiritual fulfillment in Eastern practices or in a host of other traditions.

Many similarities exist among the major religions of the world. For example, Jews and Christians teach, "Do unto others as you would have them do unto you." Confucius, the founder of an ancient Chinese system of morality known as Confucianism, is still famous for his many sayings. One of them offers a similar philosophy: "What you do not want done to yourself, do not do unto others." Hindus teach, "No man does unto another that which would be repugnant to himself." Muslims are taught that true believers must love for their brother and sister what they love for themselves.

Many religions are, in fact, historically and philosophically related to one another. Jews, Christians, and Muslims believe in the same God and trace their roots back to the prophet Abraham, a spiritual spokesperson. Baha'i came out of Islam. Hinduism gave rise to Buddhism. Buddhism influenced Taoism. Sikhism was influenced by Islam and Hinduism.

Millions of people who belong to a formal religion engage in some form of spiritual activity. Anything that generates a sense of awe or way of finding union with a sacred presence may be a source of spirituality. Prayer and meditation, in which a person works to control the breathing and to focus the mind and body are spiritual exercises that help people find peace. In the United States, nearly two-thirds of religious people pray. In scientific studies, prayer and meditation have been shown to have positive health effects. Let's explore the spiritual activity and belief systems from the religions of long ago to modern spiritual practices and the wide variety of religions worldwide.

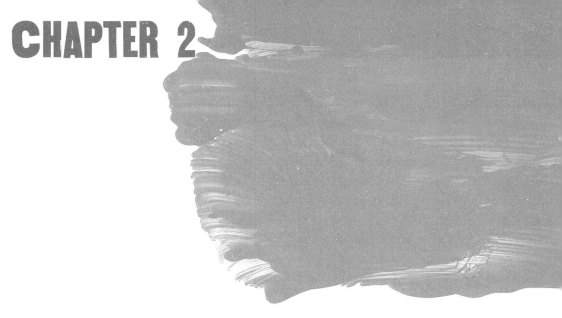

CHAPTER 2

RELIGIONS FROM THE EASTERN WORLD

You live in an age of awakened spirituality. Large numbers of people are searching for spiritual truth, and many of them are teens. Signposts point to different ways of looking at life, the inner self, reverence, and gratitude.

Many young people are exploring spirituality through different world religions. They are turning their lives away from materialism—the excessive concern with possessions. They explore many paths for a greater wealth of inner peace, love, faith, and spiritual vision.

Some of these paths, or religions, began many years ago in the eastern part of the world. Eastern religion is a group of religions originating in India, China, Japan, and Southwest Asia. Since their beginnings, the most common religions founded in the East—Hinduism, Buddhism, Jainism, Shintoism, Confucianism, Taoism, and Sikhism—have moved to many parts of the world. These religions tend to view God as within the person or have no god at all. The source of enlightenment and liberation is within the individual and in a person's proper, right relationship to their society and the universe.

Hinduism

Nan's teacher asked her to help a new girl feel at home in their eighth grade class. Nan had many friends, but this was the first time she had met someone who was Hindu. Even the new girl's name, Achai, was unfamiliar to Nan. Nan liked Achai, and she invited her to her house several times. Nan was pleased when Achai asked her to go to her house and meet her mother.

Nan was made to feel at home at Achai's house. She found the small shrine in the house interesting as well as the images of the gods that the family worshipped daily. Nan learned about Hinduism from her friend and from her teacher at school, who told the class a bit about the Hindu religion.

Hinduism is practiced by more than 80 percent of the population in India. While most Hindus live in India, substantial communities of Hindus live in Europe, Africa, and North America. Hinduism is the third most common religion in the world, with more than 850 million followers. Hindu traditions and beliefs have shaped the unique culture of India and influenced other countries where its presence is strong.

Hinduism is one of the oldest surviving religions in the world. Some forms of it date back to prehistoric times. It grew over a period of four thousand years and has no single founder or prophet. During the period between 1750 B.C. and 1200 B.C., people from what became Persia (modern-day Iran) over time moved through passes in the Himalaya Mountains into India. They were nomads—they moved across a landscape, usually seasonally, in search of food and water for their community and for their livestock. These nomadic peoples later formed cities and built minor kingdoms.

No one knows exactly when these people produced the earliest sacred books of Hinduism. Their teachings were initially transferred orally from generation to generation and were later put into writing. Some of these sacred books are known as the Vedas. A later group of sacred writings is called the Upanishads. These sacred writings contain words that are to be recited by priests at sacrifices, or offerings, to the gods; in hymns that contain basic mythology and philosophy; in rituals to be used in homes; and in popular prayers to gods or as spells to ward off evil.

One of the great epics of Hinduism is the Bhagavad Gita. It is considered by religious scholars to be among the greatest spiritual books the world has ever known. It reveals the purpose and goals of human existence. "The primary purpose of the Bhagavad-Gita is to illuminate for all of humanity the realization of the true nature of divinity; for the highest spiritual conception and the greatest material perfection is to attain love of God!" The Bhagavad Gita, which was written at least two thousand years ago, has been translated into many languages and is available in public libraries around the world and on the Internet.

Many gods and goddesses, diverse rituals, and spiritual disciplines are part of Hinduism. The gods are part of a universal spirit called Brahman—the energy or the supreme spirit that sustains all things. Many divinities make up Brahman, but they are all part of one divine essence that fills the universe. The word *Brahman* in the ancient, sacred Sanskrit language is the name for this spirit. (A Brahman is also a priest.)

In Hinduism the purpose of life is to achieve union with Brahman. Hindus aim to give up their finite, limited individuality to become part of infinity. Like paths leading up a mountain, many paths can lead to Brahman, but the peak is the goal—the soul's release from the world—to which all believers aim.

The main paths to achieve union with Brahman are five kinds of yoga. Many Americans are familiar with and practice hatha yoga, or physical yoga—a path toward concentration through bodily development.

Reincarnation is a central belief in Hinduism. Hinduism teaches that the soul never dies. When the body dies, the soul is reborn, or reincarnated, in another form, perhaps as another person or as an animal. Hindus believe that every action influences how a soul will be born in the next life. If you do evil deeds, you might come back in a lower state, perhaps in the body of a small animal. The accumulated effect of actions in this life and previous lives is known as karma.

A person's soul may pass through hundreds of rebirths before it is free to reunite with Brahman.

These reincarnations continue until a person reaches spiritual perfection, called *moksha*. From that stage of complete union with Brahman, the spirit will not return in earthly form.

Hindu Gods

Hinduism has many gods, and they take numerous forms. Their abilities, heroic deeds, and experiences are the subject of a wide range of stories. Hinduism's three main gods are Brahma, Vishnu, and Shiva. Brahma is the creator of the universe. Vishnu is the preserver of the universe. Shiva is the destroyer and

Brahma (left) *and Vishnu* (right) *are two of the gods in the Hindu trinity. These depictions are from nineteenth-century France.*

22

re-creator of the universe. While Brahman is a spirit, Brahma takes on a form. He is often depicted as having four faces and four arms and standing on a lotus flower throne.

Shiva is said to have tamed the river Ganges. The story goes that the gods wished to bestow fertility on Earth by giving it this mighty river. Shiva used his hair to break the fall of the river. This made it flow in many tributaries before the water reached one main river. Hindus believe that by bathing in the Ganges, bad deeds are forgiven. People travel from distant places to put the ashes of their relatives in the sacred water of the Ganges. Scattering ashes in the Ganges and being cremated on its banks assures the peace of heaven and better lives to come. In modern times, the water of the Ganges is highly polluted from industrial and human wastes (some of it related to riverside cremation practices). Yet bathing in the Ganges remains a purifying act for Hindus.

Stories and images of Hindu divinities are highly respected. Temple priests treat an image of a deity as an honored guest, bathing the images and presenting them with food. The images are put to bed, taken on outings, and dressed in different costumes for various celebrations. Hindus believe that a particular god, in some way, dwells in the image.

In fact, Hindus believe divinity pervades all things—plants, animals, mountains, lakes, and all other physical entities in the universe. Cows are especially valued and are animals of unique privilege. For example, cows in India and other countries with majority Hindu populations are allowed to wander through traffic in busy cities. Killing a cow and eating its beef are considered serious crimes. That's why most Hindus are vegetarians.

For many Hindus, spirituality is a large part of daily life. They worship regularly in temples, which have shrines that are each devoted to a different divinity. People worship daily at home, where they have shrines to their personal gods. Many Hindus practice ritual greetings for the rising sun and other forms of private devotion.

Hindu Social Order

Hinduism does not have a single, defined organizational structure. Acceptance of the Vedas and other sacred scriptures is one of its two most general features. The other is the distinction of social order, once known as the caste system.

Social categories provide the major division of Hindu society. Over the centuries, an individual's place in society was inherited from one generation to the next. Marriages took place within one's caste, and each group had a specific role and place in society. Yet through the years, the caste system has weakened and in some places been outlawed. For example, in India—where the caste system is officially outlawed— many Indians mix with different social orders, especially in the cities where people think and live beyond the barrier of old social systems. In small rural areas, however, the caste system continues to shape life in modern India.

In the original four castes, the priests enjoy the highest status as the Brahman, the learned interpreters of the Vedas and other sacred material. Under them in rank come the Kshatriyas, who were the regional rajas (rulers) and nobles and, in earlier eras, the warriors. Third in rank are the Vaishyas, the landowners and merchants. Lowest in rank, the Sudras are the artisans, laborers, and peasants. Each of these social orders has multiple divisions. For example, a cow herder is several levels above a tailor.

From earliest times, Hindus recognized a fifth class, known as Dalit, the untouchables. They did menial work—street cleaning, toilet cleaning, and clearing away dead bodies. They were considered so polluting that if a person from a higher caste even stepped in the shadow of an untouchable, the higher-ranked person was viewed as contaminated.

In 1950, with influence from the Indian political and spiritual leader Mohandas Gandhi, the Indian government outlawed the caste system and the mistreatment of people who were once classed as untouchables. Discrimination against untouchables has not totally ended, though. In the villages and countryside, untouchables are still outcasts. If you ask untouchables why they are in this position, they might tell you that their ancestors committed sins in their previous lives. Through the years, some Indian Hindus have rejected caste ideology by becoming Christians or Buddhists. But as many as 160 million untouchables continue to live within Hindu caste ideology.

Buddhism

Thousands of colorful lanterns line the outside of a temple in South Korea, while monks chant. Ornaments of paper lotus flowers spill onto streets. This scene occurs annually in countries that celebrate the birth of the Buddha and the existence of the religion Buddhism.

The notion that existence means human suffering is a central truth in Buddhist thought. The goal of Buddhism is to end this spiritual suffering by reaching a state of mind free from desires and other human passions. In this freer state, individuals can more truly understand the nature of life. These ideas, as well as others that create the basis for Buddhism, were first formed by Siddhartha Gautama, the man who formed Buddhism through his teachings and who became known as the Buddha.

Siddhartha Gautama was born about 500 B.C. into a wealthy and powerful Hindu royal family in the country currently known as Nepal. The Buddha was not born with this honorific title, which means "awakened one." He earned the title Buddha at the age of thirty-five when he became enlightened, a state of being awake to the true nature of existence and the way to end suffering.

Though the details of Siddhartha's journey from childhood to enlightenment vary, most of the events are similar in all accounts of the story. Buddhists believe that soon after Siddhartha was born, a prophet predicted that the baby would become either a great ruler or a holy man. He was born into a life of privilege—his parents were a king and queen. They hoped he would become a king, and they sheltered him from anything unpleasant in the world. He was never exposed to suffering or the world outside his palace. Siddhartha led a protected life and was given anything he desired. Yet he felt something was missing.

When he was twenty-nine years old, Siddhartha ventured out into the streets and saw life outside the palace for the first time. He became aware of the suffering of life as he witnessed the Four Passing Sights: old age, sickness, death, and a holy man. After experiencing these four sights, Siddhartha left his wealth and family and searched for the meaning of life and an end to suffering.

Siddhartha spent the first six years of his journey learning to meditate and practicing an ascetic lifestyle (strict self-denial). He denied himself food to the point of near starvation. After recalling a memory of his peaceful childhood, Siddhartha decided to change his path. He ate a little food he received from a passing child. After gaining some strength, he promised himself he would sit under what became known as the Bodhi Tree until he understood the meaning of life and found the end of suffering. Twenty-four hours later, after experiencing intense desire, discomfort, and doubt, Siddhartha felt that he understood the true nature of life and suffering. He became enlightened and earned the title Buddha.

After the Buddha's night under the Bodhi Tree, he chose to share his knowledge and began teaching. He wandered from village to village and taught his way of life for forty-five years. The Buddha gathered many followers along the way, and his teachings became the central focus of Buddhism.

The Buddha taught what he called the Four Noble Truths. He taught that life is full of dissatisfaction and suffering, which is ultimately caused by craving. However, it is possible to end such suffering by following what the Buddha called the Noble Eightfold Path.

The Four Noble Truths are the foundation of Buddhism and provide a unifying connection between the

This traditional mural painting from Mahabodhi Temple in Sarnath, India, shows Siddhartha Gautama (Buddha) as a young man meditating to attain enlightenment.

different schools of Buddhist thought. These truths are:

1. *Suffering, or Dukkha:* The first noble truth is that suffering, or *dukkha*, is an inevitable part of life. Suffering includes being unhappy, frustrated, discontented, feeling grief, or being in physical pain. Essentially, life is full of physical, emotional, and mental suffering.

2. *Craving, or Tanha:* The second noble truth explains the origin of suffering. The reason that we suffer is because we constantly crave things. We desire things we think will make us happy,

and we try to avoid experiences that may cause us to be uncomfortable or to feel discontented. This kind of craving, which can never be satisfied, causes suffering.

3. *End of Suffering, or Nirvana:* The third noble truth gives the first glimpse of hope. The Buddha teaches that there is an end to the suffering of life when we pursue the right path.

4. *The Noble Eightfold Path:* The fourth noble truth describes the way to attain nirvana. The Noble Eightfold Path is a guideline for Buddhist practice and lifestyle. Following the Eightfold Path is the way to end suffering.

Many Buddhists simplify the Noble Eightfold Path into the categories of wisdom, morality (or virtuous behavior), and meditation (mental discipline). This path toward nirvana is described as the Middle Way—a way of living in the middle of extremes. Living between extremes applies to actions, behaviors, and attitudes. The Buddha realized the importance of following a path of moderation through his own experience of an extremely indulgent childhood followed by practicing extreme self-denial.

The Noble Eightfold Path includes the following recommendations for a life path that will lead to the end of suffering. Each of the elements is defined in terms of its "rightness," or the right way to end the suffering of life:

1. Right View—the knowledge of truth
2. Right Intention—the intention to resist evil
3. Right Speech—saying nothing to hurt others

4. Right Action—not stealing or cheating
5. Right Livelihood—earning a living that does not cause harm to others
6. Right Effort—developing positive thought
7. Right Mindfulness—being aware of acts and thoughts that affect the world now and in the future
8. Right Concentration—being in a state of peace

The steps of right mindfulness and right concentration are associated with the Buddhist practice of meditation. Meditation is an essential component of Buddhism, as it is a method by which many Buddhists practice and reflect on the teachings of Buddha. Meditation varies in its purpose, effect, and practice, but it is vital on the path to gaining enlightenment.

As in Hinduism, the concept of karma is central to Buddhism. The idea is that every action has a result. No one can escape the consequences of choices because actions always have an effect. If the action is positive, the result will also be positive, and if the action is negative, the result will be negative.

Karma is not as simple as it seems, however. The result of an action is not immediate or obvious. Buddhists believe that karma acts as a kind of scale, where both positive and negative actions can build up, balance, and influence each other and the outcome of the actions. Karma also influences reincarnation, another basic belief of Buddhism that comes from Hinduism. (Unlike Hinduism, Buddhism does not worship deities or practice caste divisions.)

After the Buddha's death in 483 B.C., Buddhism spread. Eventually, several schools of Buddhism, which

TIBETAN BUDDHISM AND THE DALAI LAMA

Ceremony and ritual play a large role in Tibetan Buddhism. This sect has placed special emphasis on the state of consciousness at the time of death. *The Tibetan Book of the Dead* is famous even among people who know little about Buddhism. Among other things, it tells about the monks who are specially trained to guide the departing toward a higher rebirth.

His Holiness, the fourteenth Dalai Lama, is the head of state and the spiritual leader of the Tibetan people. After the Chinese invaded Tibet in 1950 and suppressed Buddhism, the Dalai Lama made his home in India. India is host to the largest Tibetan refugee population in the world. They remain in India because the Chinese rule their homeland.

His Holiness has been awarded many degrees and other honors for his efforts in the solution of internal conflicts, human rights issues, and world peace. On December 10, 1989, he accepted the Nobel Peace Prize.

The Dalai Lama has written many books on Buddhist spirituality. His book *The Universe in a Single Atom: The Convergence of Science and Spirituality* (2005) explores how the relationship between science and spirituality can lead to happiness, joy, contentment, and the alleviation of suffering of the individual and society as a whole.

hold different interpretations of the Buddha's teachings, developed throughout many countries in Asia.

Buddhism is the fourth most common religion in the world. The vast majority of Buddhists live in eastern and Southeast Asia. At least 1.5 million Buddhists live in the United States, and the number may be twice that high. Zen Buddhism, a Japanese branch, is especially popular in the United States.

Jainism

A monk named Mahavira (599 B.C.–527 B.C.), which means "Great Hero," lived in India about the same time as Buddha. Like Buddha, Mahavira grew up in great luxury. But when he was thirty years old, he left his wife and child and became a wondering ascetic and monk. He taught Jainism, a religion that had been practiced, mainly in India, for at least a few thousand years. He was the last and the most important of the Jain teachers, known as Tirthankaras.

Mahavira taught the five vows that Jain monks and nuns still take. These vows are sometimes translated as nonviolence (never causing harm to living beings), truthfulness (always speaking the harmless truth), nonstealing (never taking anything not properly given), chastity (never indulging sensual pleasure), and nonpossessionism (avoiding attachment to material places, people, and things). Jains believe that Mahavira wore one garment for more than a year, and then he walked around "sky clad" (naked), completely removed from material possessions. At the age of forty-two, Mahavira reached the highest state of enlightenment. He lived until he was seventy-two.

According to Jainism, people are born, live their lives, die, and are born again. They consider the world to be comprised of soul and matter. Soul is life, and matter is material and evil. Flesh traps the spirit, and as long as the soul is enmeshed in matter, it cannot

*This thirteenth-century Indian sculpture
shows Mahavira in meditation.*

be free. Jains believe the soul can be freed from matter only by the way a person lives life. To liberate the soul from matter, a person must practice asceticism. Those who live totally pure lives, like Mahavira, may be released from the cycle of life, death, and rebirth.

Jains believe they are trapped in the material world because of spiritual residue from their past lives. Any bad deeds block the soul from rising to the top of the universe like a spiritual balloon. Good deeds help to abolish the bad deeds and eventually allow the soul to reach a state of eternal spiritual bliss.

Jains also pursue ahimsa—the complete avoidance of harm to any living creature, even unintentionally. All Jains are vegetarians. Some won't eat anything that has been cooked in a pan in which meat has been cooked. Jains also do not use leather. They try to avoid anything, including words, that would be painful to others.

Devout Jains go to extremes to avoid harming living things. They might sweep a path before them as they walk to avoid stepping on any living thing in the path. They wear masks to prevent swallowing insects that might fly into their mouths as they breathe. Many Jains work in cities, since farming involves the unintentional killing of earthworms and other life-forms.

Jains have established many schools, hospitals, clinics, orphanages, and rehabilitation camps for the handicapped, sick, and disadvantaged. They also have hospitals for ailing birds and other animals. Donating time and money is part of the Jain belief in social obligation.

Jains do not believe in a god who created humanity. They believe that many gods are self-realized individuals who have attained liberation. Jainism strives for the realization of the highest perfection of humans.

In the twenty-first century, the majority of Jains live in India, mostly in the states of Gujarat and Maharashtra. About 100,000 Jains live in the United States and other countries. Figures for the total number of Jains vary from 4.5 million to 7.5 million. Jainism's principle of not harming life is said to have influenced many people, including twentieth-century figures such as the famous Hindu leader Mohandas Gandhi, known as the Mahatma (Great Soul), and Albert Schweitzer (1875–1965), a humanitarian and Nobel laureate from France.

Shintoism

Myoko carries her baby to the shrine where the baby is placed under the protection of the *kami*—spirits that inhabit the natural world. Myoko purifies herself by washing her mouth and her hands with water from the spring nearby. Then she bows before the shrine. Myoko presents food offerings, and the priest says prayers. Myoko's family and friends join in the service. The ritual is carried out in a spirit of cheerfulness, sincerity, and purity. Music and dance are part of the ceremony. After the ceremony, family and friends drink a rice wine called sake, a common practice in Japan at celebrations.

For many modern Japanese people, Shinto is a matter of custom and tradition. In taking her baby to the shrine, Myoko is observing the Shinto tradition of observing the child's first shrine visit on the thirty-second day after birth for a boy (and the thirty-third day for a girl). Traditionally, a baby was taken to the shrine by a grandmother because by going through childbirth, the mother was thought to be impure. In modern times, however, the child is often taken by the mother.

As a religion, Shinto continues a love of the natural landscape of Japan and the world. Shinto worships the spirits in nature. In fact, Shinto means the "way of the kami." Kami can reside in human beings and other animals—such as squirrels, butterflies, and frogs—and in trees, mountains, rocks, and more. These spirits inhabit much of the natural world. The most widely worshipped of all kami is the sun goddess, Amaterasu. She is regarded as the mother goddess of Japan. This goddess was considered the founder of the Japanese imperial family, which was believed to be divine. All the Japanese emperors are descended from this line.

Although Shinto beliefs and ways of thinking are part of the lives of many Japanese people, Shinto has no leader, no holy book, and no canon (official body of teachings). Shinto had its origins in prehistoric times. It became the official religion of Japan beginning in 1889, when the state took over the care of 110,000 shrines with about sixty thousand priests to tend them. The shrines were spread throughout the country, and each one was dedicated to a god or goddess.

Every Shinto shrine has at least one gateway, known as a torii. These gates are built with two upright side pieces and one elaborate crosspiece. The wood is either left natural or painted red. Some shrines have many torii, forming a line of gateways. The temple itself often houses a metallic mirror that represents the sun goddess. Shrines often contain water for ritual purification of hands and mouth. Each time practitioners of Shinto go to a shrine to pray, they must be purified by rinsing their mouths with water and by washing their hands before they enter the shrine.

Japan's many Shinto shrines are visited regularly by local believers, and special shrine days are celebrated. Numerous festivals are held at shrines throughout the year. Shinto is a system of traditional

The Itsukushima Shrine (above) *was built in the thirteenth century. Many people visit Shinto shrines throughout Japan each year.*

rituals and ceremonies for about four million people in Japan.

Confucianism

Selma's grandmother is ninety-five years old. The two go on walks together, but because Selma's grandmother can't walk very fast, they move slowly. Selma's friends tease her for respecting her grandmother and helping her no matter how it interferes with Selma's life. But Selma always treats her grandmother in a dignified manner because she has grown up in a family that follows the philosophy of Confucianism. Selma is a gentle Chinese woman with reverence and respect for all the members of her family, her friends, and the rest of the world. Confucianism plays a major role in the rites of passage and moral behavior in public life in China.

Confucius was born in China in the sixth century B.C. He was a great teacher who saw humans as social creatures bound to one another with human kindness. He expressed the importance of five relationships— ruler and subject, parent and child, elder and younger brother, husband and wife, and friend and friend. He believed that in relations where one person is superior

This image of Confucius was created in seventeenth-century China.

to the other, the superior person must treat the inferior person with respect.

Confucianism has shaped China for more almost 2,500 years. The teachings were spread by its disciples. It reached Japan, Korea, Vietnam, and many other countries. But because Confucianism does not teach a belief in gods or life after death, it is not always considered to be a religion. Some people view it as an ethical system, which defines personal behavior and relationships in an ideal moral order.

Confucian political and moral ideas are sometimes expressed in short sayings, compiled in various books and available on the Internet. A few examples are:

He who studies but does not think is lost; he who thinks but does not study is dangerous.
A journey of a thousand miles begins with the first step.
Do not do unto others what you would not want others to do unto you.

Some followers of Confucianism practice more than one belief system. They may describe themselves as followers of Confucianism, Buddhism, Taoism, or a mix of these. Several religions often overlap. These religions are not intolerant of one another.

Taoism

Taoism, along with Buddhism and Confucianism, became one of the three great religions of China. Taoism (Daoism), sometimes known as the "other way," is an interpretation of nature worship that values practices leading to happiness and harmony. Developed in China in the sixth through fourth century B.C., Taoism is the basis of a spiritual approach to living. It follows the creative path of nature, not the values of human society. For example, Taoism sees artistic creation as an expression of inner spiritual feelings rather than coming from a desire for monetary rewards. Or a person tired of the stresses of her work life retires to the countryside to commune with nature. A very old story known as "Peach Blossom Spring" is often used to illustrate the Tao approach to life:

A fisher who lived in a mountainous region of China discovered a river with peach blossoms scattered along the banks. The river led him to a hidden valley where people had lived for centuries without contact with the outside world. They lived simple lives in harmony with one another and oblivious to the turmoil of the world beyond their community. They begged the fisher to stay with them, but he left so that he could share his discovery with his friends. When he tried to return to the peaceful village, he could not find it. He did not realize that to find the village he would have to travel a spiritual path, rather than a physical path. It was a state of mind that made his utopia.

The founder of Taoism is believed to be Lao-tzu (sixth century B.C.), a contemporary of Confucius. Lao-tzu's book, *Tao Te Ching,* is usually translated into English as "The Way and the Power" and is considered a spiritual classic. It has been translated into many different languages, including English. Taoism borrowed much from Buddhism. It is seen as an alternative to Confucianism, a philosophy sometimes regarded as strict and logical, while Taoism is often viewed as emotional, magical, and

This Chinese scroll painting shows Lao-tzu, the founder of Taoism.

not concerned with rational logic. However, a person may practice Confucianism and Taoism at different phases in life or value them for the way they speak to different sides of the human personality.

Taoism is concerned with healing and vitality. Many exercises and movements are related to Taoism. For example, tai chi is a form of exercise with specific dance-like meditative movements. Tai chi is believed to balance the energy flow in the body. It works on all parts of the body, stimulating the central nervous system, lowering blood pressure, relieving stress, toning muscles without strain, and generally improving function of internal organs. *Qigong* (also called *chi kung*) is another Taoist practice that involves physical movements and certain breathing patterns with similar benefits.

Yin and yang is a well-known Taoist symbol, also called Taijitu. It represents the balance of opposites in the universe. The two interlocking swirling shapes (one white and one black) in the yin and yang circle give the impression of change, the only constant factor in the universe. The shapes are associated with the masculine and the feminine, the dark and the light, the strong and the weak, and many other complementary opposites. Since nothing in nature is purely black or white, the white swirl has a small black spot and the black swirl has a small white spot.

Sikhism

Sapreet is a young man in India who wears a turban made of several yards of yellow cloth. He wraps the cloth neatly around his head, covering his long hair. Sikh men do not cut the hair on their heads, and they have moustaches and beards. It is difficult for Sapreet to ride his motorcycle to work every day because the law says he must wear a metal helmet for safety. Sapreet feels strongly about wearing his turban, and yet he cannot fit the helmet over it.

The turban is part of Sapreet's religious tradition. He says he should not be fined for not wearing a helmet. He has decided to go to court to contest the law. He asks his friends to write blogs in his favor.

The turban is a requirement for men and women of the Sikh faith, for it symbolizes discipline, integrity, humility, and spirituality. Yet, many modern Sikh men and women don't wear the turban. Because of peer pressure, many young Sikh males have cut their hair and do not wear the turbans that contain it.

A Sikh boy shops at a store in India. People of the Sikh faith are required to wear turbans, although many do not.

Sikhism is the world's fifth-largest organized religion. About 25 million Sikhs live around the world, with about 1 million in North America. Sikhs make up about 2 percent of the people living in India, where the religion began.

The Beginning of Sikhism

About five hundred years ago, a man named Nanak (1469–1539) was born to a Hindu family in the Punjab region of northwestern India, where both Hindus and Muslims lived. Nanak married at the age of nineteen and fathered two children. When he was nearly thirty years old, Nanak left his family to work in the city of Sultanpur. There he made a habit of meditating in the forest nearby. He and his friends formed a group who worshipped and meditated by the side of a river.

One day, Nanak's clothes were found by the side of the river. He disappeared for three days. During that time, he had a vision from God informing him that he was to be a prophet of the "true religion." When he returned to his family, he remained silent for a day before making the enigmatic pronouncement: "There is neither Hindu nor Muslim, so whose path shall I follow? I shall follow God's path." Nanak believed that God was a formless spiritual force shared by all religions.

For the next twenty years, Nanak traveled widely, encouraging men and women to follow his new religion. Nanak taught his message to numerous people, who became known as Sikhs, a word meaning "disciples" or "learners." For Nanak and his followers, the true religion represents a spiritual path to God.

Sikhism was not always tolerated in India. An armed struggle took place between the Sikhs and Muslim emperors in India during the eighteenth century. The Sikhs managed to maintain an independent kingdom in the Punjab region until 1849, when the British took over the region. In 1925 the Sikhs regained control of their temples, many of which had been under Hindu control. In 1947, when India gained its independence from Great Britain, the western Punjab became part of Pakistan (a majority Muslim nation). About two million Sikhs fled the Punjab, while about the same number of Muslims made their way to Pakistan from other parts of India. During the exchange of population, violence was rampant and many people were killed and injured.

Spirituality of Sikhism

Sikhs believe in one formless God, whose name is Truth. He is the creator. He is fearless, without hate, and beyond birth and death. Sikhs are prohibited from worshipping idols, images, or icons. Only God can be worshipped.

Sikhs believe in freedom of speech and of religion, justice and liberty for all, and absolute equality of all people without regard to gender, race, caste, or religion. All Sikh males share the name Singh (lion). It was traditionally used as a family name, but many modern Sikhs use it as a middle name. Women have the name Kaur, which means "princess." The naming practice is meant to signify equality among people, as opposed to the caste system that was common throughout most of India. Sikhs reject the caste system. They believe in equality for women and men and emphasize community service and helping the needy.

Sikhs express their spirituality through selfless service to humanity. The three main principles are living a pure, honest life and being fair in all personal and professional dealings; meditating on the name of God; and sharing through charitable work. Regardless of their social position, Sikhs are always conscious of the needs of others. Whether it is food, clothing, shelter, or a basic right that is being denied, Sikhs are always prepared to give their time and money to guarantee that these requirements are met.

The writings of Nanak and the nine gurus (teachers) who followed him, numerous hymns, and some of the writings of Hindu and Muslim saints (holy people) are recorded in the Sri Guru Granth Sahib (Book of God). This book has 1,430 pages and contains more than five thousand hymns. It is treated with the same respect as a person. This sacred scripture has its own room in any Sikh temple, and whenever it is moved, it is attended by five Sikhs.

A distinct feature of the Sikh religion is a common kitchen, called a *langar*, in each Sikh temple. The worshippers bring food or money for a meal that is eaten after the service in the temple. Anyone who wishes to participate in the free meal may do so. In Delhi, India, thirty thousand people eat in one langar daily, and the number swells to one hundred thousand

FREEDOM OF RELIGION

About 10 percent of the twenty-five thousand Sikhs who live in Canada are orthodox (those who strictly observe the rituals of the religion) and follow the five articles of faith. One twelve-year-old boy who followed the five clothing practices was challenged by the administration of his school in Quebec after he dropped his *kirpan* at recess. Knives were forbidden in the school, and the school officials were concerned about the possibility of violence. Yet, Sikhism prohibits the use of the kirpan as a weapon.

In a five-year court battle, the case reached the Supreme Court of Canada, where it was tried in 2006. The court ruled in favor of the boy and noted the importance of protecting freedom of religion and respect for minorities. Some restrictions were put in place about wearing the ceremonial knife, however. For example, the kirpan can be no longer than 7 inches (18 centimeters) and must be secured in a sheath. The wearer must be a baptized member of the Sikh faith.

each Sunday, the most common day for public worship. Sikhs sit on the floor while eating their meals to emphasize that all people are equal. The religion forbids smoking and drinking alcoholic beverages.

Devout Sikh men in different parts of the world follow the same five articles of faith, the five Ks:

1. Hair is never cut. This is called *kes.* Sikh men gather their hair on their heads under a turban. Moustaches and beards are worn but are often trimmed.
2. A comb, the *kangha,* is carried to keep the hair in place.
3. A small sword or dagger is carried as a symbol to remind the Sikh of the need to fight against oppression in any form. The sword is called a *kirpan.*
4. A steel bangle, the *kara,* forms a circle that symbolizes one God without beginning or end. It is worn as a bracelet.
5. Breeches, called *kaccha,* are worn under robes. They symbolize readiness to ride into battle or help in an emergency. In modern times, they are often worn as underwear.

Although most Sikhs live in India, others live in many countries around the world. They are so widespread that Sikhs like to tell a joke about U.S. astronaut Neil Armstrong when he landed on the moon in 1969. They say Armstrong was dismayed when a Sikh taxi driver—who was already on the moon—drove up to him and asked, "Where to, Sir?"

CHAPTER 3

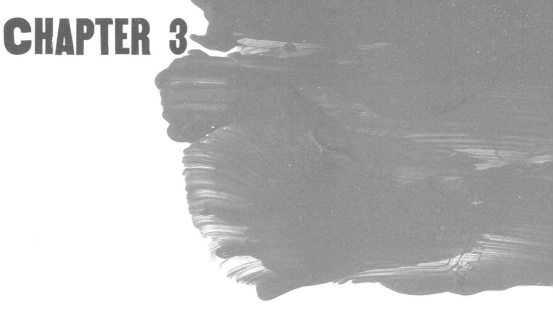

ABRAHAMIC RELIGIONS

Several of the world's major religions began with a man named Abraham. Known as Ibrahim in Arabic, this prophet of God is an important figure in the Hebrew Bible of the Jews, the Old Testament of the Christians, and the Quran of the Muslims. Bahaism—an offshoot of Islam—is also an Abrahamic religion.

The major organized Abrahamic religions are monotheisms. Their adherents believe in only one God—a formless, spiritual force. In contrast to Eastern religions, where reincarnation is a common belief, Abrahamic religions teach that people live on Earth only once. They also believe in life after death, but unlike the philosophy of reincarnation, it is not a return to physical life on Earth.

Judaism

Twelve-year-old Rachael kisses a small box on the doorframe as she leaves her house. The box holds fifteen verses from the Bible. The box is called a mezuzah. It signifies that Rachael's home is Jewish and that her family believes in the God of Abraham as the creator and sustainer of the universe. Other doors in Rachael's house have mezuzahs too. They are there to remind everyone to follow God's laws every time they enter or leave a room. Rachael's family says a prayer each morning and evening. This prayer begins, "Hear, O Israel, the Lord Our God, the Lord is One." Rachael goes to classes at her synagogue, a Jewish house of worship. There, she learns more about God's laws and prepares for her bat mitzvah. This ceremony will mark her thirteenth birthday, when she will be considered an adult in the Jewish community.

A Jewish boy (second from left) goes through the steps of his bar mitzvah. A bar mitzvah is the male version of a bat mitzvah. Bar means "son" and bat means "daughter" in Aramaic and Hebrew.

The God of Israel

Jewish law forbids Jews to make images of God (such as paintings or sculptures), because God has no physical form. God is a spirit. Since God has no body, God is neither male nor female. Jewish writings sometimes tell of God speaking and mention God's hand or heart. But these references are considered figures of speech and are not taken literally.

According to Jewish teaching, God has no beginning and no end. God exists in the past, the present, and the future. God is everywhere.

The Founding of Judaism

Abraham lived about four thousand years ago. God promised to bless the descendants of Abraham and promised the land of Israel—land at the eastern end of the Mediterranean Sea—to his children. The Jews trace their ancestry to Abraham's son Isaac and Isaac's son Jacob.

According to the Bible, Jacob had twelve sons, who founded the Twelve Tribes of Israel, or Israelites. The Israelites migrated to Egypt, where they were enslaved. Moses, a prophet and a descendant of Abraham, was instructed by God to say to the pharaoh (ruler of Egypt), "Let my people go." When the pharaoh refused, God sent ten plagues to the Egyptians, and the pharaoh was overwhelmed. After the tenth plague, he let the people go. But he changed his mind and sent an army in pursuit of them. At the shores of the Red Sea, God parted the waters so the Israelites could cross, but when the Egyptian soldiers tried to follow them, they were drowned.

At Mount Sinai, at the head of the Red Sea, God gave Moses stone tablets. The stone tablets contained a set of laws, called the Ten Commandments. The commandments tell how people should relate to one another and God. The commandments are:

1. You shall have no other gods before me.
2. You shall not make graven images [idols], bow down to them, or serve them.
3. You shall not take the name of the Lord, your God, in vain [use it in swearing].
4. Observe the Sabbath day to keep it holy. Six days shall you labor and do all your work, but the seventh day is a Sabbath to the Lord thy God; in it you shall not do any work.
5. You shall honor your father and mother.
6. You shall not murder.
7. Neither shall you commit adultery [be unfaithful to a spouse].
8. Neither shall you steal.
9. Neither shall you bear false witness against your neighbor [spread untruths about others].
10. Neither shall you covet [desire] your neighbor's wife, or anything that is your neighbor's.

God also gave Moses the Torah, the first five books of the Hebrew Bible. The word *Torah* is sometimes used to mean the whole Hebrew Bible. (Christians call it the Old Testament). After the first five books of the Bible, the history of the Jewish people follows. The prophets, such as Isaiah and Jeremiah, were spokespeople for God to the people and to their leaders. The Psalms express poems and hymns of the Hebrew people. Through the ages, many people have found comfort and joy from the Psalms. The Book of Proverbs includes many points of wisdom. For example: "He that is slow to anger is better than the mighty and he that rules his spirit than he that takes a city."

Jewish Law and Beliefs

Jewish law is compiled in several written sources, including the Hebrew Bible. In about the second century A.D., Jewish scholars wrote down oral law (laws passed down through word of mouth) in a document called the Mishnah. Explanations of the laws (known as the Gemara) were added later. These two collections compose the Talmud, an important body of Jewish law.

Moses ben Maimon (also known as Maimonides) was a twelfth-century Jewish scholar who was born in Spain and settled in Egypt. He created a list of thirteen principles of Jewish faith:

1. God exists.
2. God is one and unique.
3. God is incorporeal [not composed of matter].
4. God is eternal.
5. Prayer is to be directed to God alone and no other.
6. The words of the prophets are true.
7. Moses's prophecies are true, and Moses was the greatest of all prophets.
8. The written Torah and oral Torah [teachings contained in the Talmud and other writings] were given to Moses.
9. There will be no other Torah.

10. God knows the thoughts and deeds of men.
11. God will reward the good and punish the wicked.
12. The Messiah [the expected king and deliverer of the Jews] will come.
13. The dead will be resurrected.

The Jewish People

Originally, Jews were a loosely connected people, with twelve tribes named after the twelve sons of Jacob. According to the Torah, God made a promise to King David—king of Israel for forty years until 837 B.C.—that a descendant of his would always be on the throne of Israel.

By the Middle Ages (500–1500), Jews were scattered throughout Europe, North Africa, and the Middle East. In the nineteenth and twentieth centuries, many Jews migrated to the United States.

In the years before World War II (1939–1945), the German leader Adolf Hitler wanted to rid his country of Jews. Hitler claimed that Jews were an inferior race. Hitler's Nazis began to send European Jews to death camps. Six million Jews, more than one-third of the Jews in the world at that time, were murdered or died of disease or starvation in the Nazi camps. This systematic killing of Jews is called the Holocaust.

After the war, many Jews wanted to return to their ancestral homeland in Israel. In 1947 the United Nations—an international organization for peace—agreed to the creation of a Jewish state in Israel. But many Arab Muslims also lived in this land. The United Nations divided the territory into a Jewish state, called the State of Israel, and an Arab section. Years of violent boundary disputes followed.

In the twenty-first century, about 37 percent of the world's Jews live in Israel. More than 44 percent live in North America, and 12 percent live in Europe. Others live in various countries, making a total of about 15 million Jews around the world.

Modern Jewish Life

Modern Jews practice their faith by worshipping in synagogues, observing Jewish holidays, and performing other rites, such as bar mitzvah ceremonies for boys and bat mitzvah ceremonies for girls. In synagogue, to show reverence to God, Jewish men wear small caps called yarmulkes. They may also wear talliths, or prayer shawls. Jews hold worship services in Hebrew, the language of the ancient Israelites, as well as other modern languages. Some modern Jews keep kosher—that is, they follow ancient Jewish dietary laws. Under these laws, certain foods, such as pork and shellfish, are forbidden. People who keep kosher do not eat meat and milk products at the same meal. They keep separate dishes and utensils for these different foods.

The modern Jewish community is divided into three branches—Orthodox, Conservative, and Reform. Orthodox Jews are the most observant. Religion guides every aspect of their daily lives. On the Sabbath, which begins at sundown Friday evening and continues until sundown on Saturday, Orthodox Jews do not use telephones, electricity, or automobiles or perform any kind of labor. Orthodox Jews keep kosher

An Orthodox Jewish family in Jerusalem celebrates the Sabbath.

and observe other ancient Jewish practices. Hassidic Jews are the strictest of the Orthodox Jews.

Conservative and Reform Jews are less strict about Jewish practices. Conservative Jews follow some traditional practices, but they also believe that practices can be changed to fit modern times. Reform Jews teach that the principles of Judaism are more important than the practices.

All Jews celebrate the same holidays. Rosh Hashanah is the Jewish New Year. It falls in September or October, depending on the Jewish calendar. Yom Kippur, the day of atonement, comes ten days after Rosh Hashanah. On this day, Jews fast from sundown until sundown. They ask God for forgiveness for their sins. Yom Kippur is the most important holiday of the Jewish calendar.

Another important holiday is Passover, which lasts for eight days. Passover takes place in March or April.

It celebrates the time, in biblical days, that the Jews escaped from slavery in Egypt. On Passover, people eat special foods that symbolize the flight from Egypt.

Hanukkah falls in December. This holiday commemorates a Jewish victory over a Syrian tyrant in ancient Israel. Jews celebrate Hanukkah by lighting candles for eight days.

Christianity

On a Sunday morning in the United States, Keenan is attending a Christian service. Every Sunday he goes to church, where he recites Christian prayers with the rest of the congregation. He knows the service and its rituals by heart and tries to lead a Christian life, loving others, helping those in need, and being humble.

Keenan reflects on the Christian concept of sin, or the ways in which a person fails to live up to God's expectations of moral human behavior. Keenan prays for forgiveness, praises God, and tries to live a good and useful life, helping out every Thursday night at a kitchen that serves meals to homeless people in his hometown.

Dan practices his Christian spirituality in a different way. He is less interested in expressing his spirituality through defined rituals. So he belongs to a church that is very informal and that invites the congregation to help shape weekly services. Some of their services are held in a marketplace, in a natural setting, or in an urban ghetto. Everyone is welcome, no matter what their sexual orientation, race, or former beliefs may be. Dan also participates in his church's outreach programs, which help people in need in his community.

More than two billion people around the world profess Christianity, including 80 percent of Americans. Within Christianity is a wide range of beliefs and practices. Although there are many forms of worship, all Christians believe in God as the creator of the universe.

The Christian God exists in three entities that share a single divine presence: God the Father, God the Son, and God the Holy Spirit. The three are known as the Trinity. Christians believe that the Holy Spirit lives on in every believer. God makes himself known in the lives of humans through the Holy Spirit. The Son of God is the Messiah, Jesus.

Christians believe in the writings in the Old Testament of the Bible—the Hebrew texts, including those that foretell of the Messiah. The Messiah was to be the one who, in God's plan, would purchase the freedom of people from sin and fulfill the prophecy of the coming of a savior. According to Christian belief, the Messiah is Jesus. Christians believe Jesus is the son of God who died for the sins of the world.

The New Testament of the Bible is central to the Christian faith. The first four books of the New Testament of the Bible are called Gospels. The word *gospel* means "good news." They tell about the life and death of Jesus and claim that Jesus was the Messiah. Christianity is based on the teachings, life, death, and resurrection of Jesus.

The Story of Jesus

Jesus was born a Jew about 4 B.C. and lived in Judea (present-day Israel), the home of the Jews in ancient times—also known as the Holy Land. According to traditional Christian interpretation, Jesus is the son of God, made human. God the Father sent Jesus to Earth to live as humans do. Jesus was born to Mary, wife of Joseph, a carpenter of Nazareth, Galilee.

Jesus grew up as a Jewish boy in a family that observed Jewish faith and customs. When he was about thirty, he left his home and traveled around Judea. He spent his time teaching, helping people, performing miracles, and proclaiming the Kingdom of God that will come in the future when Christ returns to Earth.

Jesus performed miracles by healing the sick and the blind, raising the dead, casting out demons, and feeding the hungry. He emphasized that faith in him played a large part in the miracles. Jesus stayed within 90 miles (145 kilometers) of his birthplace, but his followers spread his influence around the world after his death. Jesus taught the followers in many ways, but his parables (teaching stories) are especially famous.

An example of a parable is the famous story of the good Samaritan. (Samaritans are an ethnic group with historic roots in the Middle East.) When Jesus was asked, "What shall I do to inherit eternal life?" He said, "What is written in the Law? How does it read to you?" The man answered, "You shall love the Lord your God with all your heart, with all your soul, and with all your strength, and with all your mind; and your neighbor as yourself." Jesus said to him, "You have answered correctly; Do this and you will live."

Then the man questioned Jesus, "Who is my neighbor?"

So Jesus told him a story of a man who was robbed and beaten on his way from Jerusalem to Jericho. By chance a priest was going down that road, and when the priest saw the beaten man, he passed by on the other side. Priests were supposed to be ritually clean, avoiding contamination that would come through association with non-Jewish people. In approaching a wounded man who was not a Jew, the priest would have been made unclean.

Jesus continued the story and told of a Levite (a man from the Hebrew tribe of Levi) who also saw the beaten man and did not help him. But a Samaritan, who was on a journey, saw the beaten man and helped him. He bandaged his wounds, pouring healing oil and wine on them, and he put the man on his own beast and brought him to an inn and took care of him. On the next day, the Samaritan gave two days' wages to the innkeeper and told him to take care of the man. The Samaritan promised to repay the innkeeper if he needed more money.

Jesus asked his questioner, "Which of these three proved to be a neighbor of the man who fell into the robbers' hands?" And the man who had asked the question said, "The one who showed mercy toward him." And Jesus said to him, "Go and do likewise." Samaritans did not come from the area where the injured man was found, so he was not literally his neighbor. Yet the Samaritan was willing to risk defilement to help an outcast, and that made him his spiritual "neighbor."

Jesus taught people to love their enemies along with their friends. He taught them to pray for those who persecute and to love unreservedly. His teachings were focused on two important ideas: God's overwhelming love of humanity and the need for people to accept that love and let it flow through them. These and other good deeds that Jesus taught, he himself lived. The Christian Bible says his life was without sin.

The Crucifixion

The Roman Empire ruled Judea at this time. Roman leaders worried that Jesus—in his teachings about the spiritual kingdom of God—was a revolutionary who would threaten their rule. When Jesus was thirty-three, he went to teach in Jerusalem, during the holy time of Passover. When he entered the city, which was bustling with Jews marking the holiday, he was widely acclaimed by the people. They greeted him with fronds from the palm trees that were plentiful in the region. The people shouted "Hosanna," which means "Save us."

After this, Jesus taught in the temple in Jerusalem for a few days, leaving the city each afternoon to stay at the home of his friends, Mary, Martha, and Lazarus. On Thursday evening of that week, he ate a meal with his disciples. At this Jewish seder, known by Christians as the Last Supper, Jesus blessed the wine and the bread. Knowing that one of his disciples would betray him to the Romans, Jesus asked that he be remembered through the ritual of partaking of bread and wine. (Christians perform this act of remembrance—known as the Holy Communion—at their church services.) That night Jesus prayed in the Garden of Gethsemane, where his spiritual strength sustained him. Jesus's disciple Judas Iscariot did indeed betray him, and the Romans arrested Jesus.

The Romans brought Jesus to trial on Friday for his preaching. The Romans sentenced him to be crucified on a cross in the standard form of execution for criminals at that time. In line with his teachings, Jesus offered no resistance during his arrest, trial, and crucifixion, even when the Romans placed a crown of thorns on his head to mock him and torture him. His death on the cross was slow and agonizing. Christians believe that the suffering of Jesus was atonement, or payment, for the sins of humanity. Through his suffering, Jesus conquered death so that all could live again in heaven. Interpretations of this are widely discussed in modern times.

According to Christian beliefs, three days after his death on the cross, Jesus Christ arose triumphant from his tomb. This event is celebrated as Easter. Jesus had been raised from the dead by the power of God the Father. The Gospels report that the risen Jesus was seen by many followers. They believed that Jesus was the Messiah, not an earthly king but the spiritual ruler of all. The followers spread the word of the ascension (rising), when forty days after his resurrection, Jesus ascended into heaven. The resurrection and Christ as the Messiah became central to the Christian faith. One of the most succinct summaries of the Christian faith is "For God so loved the world that He gave his one and only Son, so that whoever believes in Him shall not perish but have everlasting life." This means that the faithful will live forever in heaven.

Christianity Spreads

The new religion of Christianity spread rapidly throughout the Roman Empire. The earliest Christians were born and raised under Judaism, and many were persecuted (officially repressed) for their beliefs. The most common reason for the persecution of thousands of the early Christians was their refusal to worship the Roman emperors as gods. Their preaching about the establishment of the Kingdom of God was considered a rebellion against the authority of the government, which was a criminal offense, punishable by death, in the Roman Empire.

As a result, many early Christians were persecuted or put to death. For example, Jesus' disciples Peter and John, along with other apostles, were imprisoned under Roman leadership. Paul, who was important in spreading the gospel, was among the many who were persecuted. Because of this, early Christians met secretly in private homes and in underground passages and rooms called catacombs. A sign—a simple outline of a fish—led many Christians to these secret places of worship. The fish represents Jesus.

In the second, third, and fourth centuries A.D., Christianity became stronger and more widespread. Roman emperor Constantine gave his support to Christianity in 313, and by the end of the fourth century, Christianity had become the state religion of the Roman Empire.

Through the centuries, Christians established communities in many parts of the world. Various Christian military and religious wars known as the Crusades took place between the eleventh and thirteenth centuries. The Crusades were led by European Christians in an attempt to regain the Holy Land from Muslim control.

Christianity eventually spread across the world. It developed into an enormously influential institution.

CHRISTIANITY DIVIDES

The first great division of the Christian Church occurred in A.D. 320, when the Eastern Orthodox Church split with the Roman Catholic Church, centered in Rome. The capital of the Roman Empire moved to Constantinople (modern Istanbul, Turkey), and Eastern Christianity established its headquarters there. Language, culture, geography, and politics influenced the split.

The next great division appeared in western Europe in the sixteenth century, when Protestants split from the Roman Catholic Church. In this century, a German monk named Martin Luther and others rebelled against some of the practices of the Catholic Church, in what became known as the Reformation. Over time, Protestants formed a variety of different Christian denominations. These vary in Christian philosophies and practices. Baptists, Lutherans, and Calvinists are just a few of the approximately thirty-four thousand active Protestant denominations, which also include Evangelical Christianity.

In the twenty-first century, 2.1 billion people around the globe are Christians. The ways of Christian worship in modern times vary from those who live solitary lives in monasteries to members of megachurches, where many thousands attend services and other activities each week. Places of worship vary from house churches, where a group gathers in someone's home, to magnificent cathedrals.

While attendance has decreased at many mainline Christian churches in Europe and the United States, Christianity is growing in Africa. In 1900 about 10

*About twelve thousand Christians worship
at a new megachurch in Guatemala.*

million people in Africa were Christians. In the 2000s,
about 360 million Africans—about one-third the population of the African continent—are Christians.

Islam

About 1.6 billion people are Muslims and practice the
faith of Islam. Five times a day, in various places around
the world, a muezzin, or crier, calls Muslims to prayer.
From a minaret, a high tower of a mosque, or by elec-
tronic recording, Muslims hear the call to prayer, and in
response, they praise Allah, the Arabic word for "God"
(the same God that Christians and Jews worship). Five

times a day—at dawn, noon, midafternoon, sunset, and evening—faithful Muslims bow to Allah, facing the holy city of Mecca, Saudi Arabia. Mecca is the birthplace of the prophet Muhammad, the founder of the religion of Islam. The muezzin announces in Arabic:

God is most great.
God is most great.
I testify that there is no god but God.
I testify that Muhammad is the Prophet of God.
Arise and pray.
God is most great.
God is most great.
There is no god but God.

During a soccer game, a team from a Muslim school calls time-out at prayer time. They go to the side of the field, unroll their prayer mats, and remove their shoes. They clear their minds of the soccer game, cleanse their minds and hearts of all worldly thoughts, and concentrate on God and the blessings he has given them. They wash their hands, feet, and arms up to the elbows with water from a bucket that has been left at the side of the field. They are ready to enter the presence of God with a clean mind and clean body.

Then they stand facing Mecca. They begin the prayers with hands raised to the level of their ears while they silently proclaim the greatness of God. With hands folded over their stomachs or chests, they remain standing while they recite passages that they have memorized from the Quran (the holy book of Islam). Then they bow to show respect and love for God and proclaim three times: "Glory to God in the

Highest." They return to the upright position and then prostrate themselves, lowering their heads to the ground with foreheads touching the prayer mat, to show submission. They recite "Glory to the Lord Most High," as they sit back on their heels three times to show acceptance.

They prostrate themselves again before standing. Prayers also include reciting, "There is no god but God and Muhammad is the Messenger of God." At the end when they stand, they say, "May the peace, mercy and blessings of God be upon you." When their prayers are finished, the team members roll up their prayer mats, put them back on the side of the field, and continue playing soccer.

This observation of prayer is called Salat. It is one of the five pillars of faith, or holy duties, in Islam. The

A Muslim man prays during a break in his soccer match in Afghanistan.

other four pillars are to declare that there is none worthy of worship except Allah and that the prophet Muhammad is the Messenger of Allah; to pay *zakat* (alms—give money to the poor); to make a pilgrimage (holy journey) to Mecca to the Great Mosque at least once, if possible; and to observe fasting from food and drink from dawn to dusk during the holy month of Ramadan.

The pilgrimage to Mecca, Saudi Arabia, known as the hajj, is required at least once in the lifetime of Muslims who are well enough and can afford the journey. The pilgrimage—a supreme form of worship—is a journey of spiritual healing that may involve many days of travel. The trips are spent in almost constant prayer. About 2.5 million Muslims from more than 160 countries go to Mecca each year, where they make the ascent to Mount Arafat to pray for salvation. Although women may participate in the hajj, most pilgrims are men.

Before entering Mecca, the pilgrims purify themselves. They bathe, set aside their everyday clothes, and wear a simple white garment to show their equality with others and their humility before God. Men wear two unstitched, white, seamless cloths, one draped over the left shoulder and one around the waist, falling to their ankles. Women wear a modified version of the two white cloths, or modest dresses, that cover everything except their feet, face, and hands. The pilgrims walk over a prescribed path and refrain from food, drink, and sex during the daylight hours until the tenth day of the hajj.

The pilgrimage celebrates particular events in the history of Islam and involves several key rituals.

One of these is to circle the Kaaba seven times. The Kaaba is a cube-shaped building inside the al-Masjid al-Haram mosque in Mecca. Muslims consider this the most sacred place on Earth. The Kaaba is the shrine that holds the sacred Black Stone, the al-Hajar-ul-Aswad, that God is said to have given to Adam, the world's first man. Muslims believe that the stone was originally white and that it turned black by absorbing the sins of all the pilgrims who touched it. Another important ritual of the pilgrimage involves throwing pebbles at three walls called *jamarat* in the city of Mina just east of Mecca. These walls symbolize the devil. After ten days, many pilgrims celebrate for the next three days.

Muslim worshippers gather around the Kaaba in Mecca. During the hajj pilgrimage, even more worshippers surround the Kaaba.

The Story of Muhammad

Muslim spirituality is rooted in the Quran. The Quran contains many legends and traditions that parallel the Bible. Muslims believe that only the Quran contains the complete expression of God's actual words, as dictated by the prophet Muhammad in Arabic.

Muhammad was born in A.D. 570 in Mecca. As he was growing up, he was known for his honesty and trustworthiness. A wealthy widow named Khadija, who was fifteen years older, employed him. Gradually their relationship grew into love. They married and had children.

Muhammad was concerned about the relaxed moral standards of his neighbors and about their belief in many gods. He often spent long periods of time meditating. About fifteen years after he was married, on one of the many nights he spent meditating in a cave, Muhammad was visited by the angel Gabriel in the form of a man. He had a vision in which the angel ordered him "to recite." According to tradition, Gabriel brought the following message:

> Recite: In the name of the Lord who created,
>   created Man of a blood clot,
> Recite: And thy lord is the Most Generous,
>   who taught by the Pen,
>   taught man what he knew not.

Muhammad was frightened, but he accepted the call to proclaim the word of God. His wife was the first convert to the religion of Islam. At frequent intervals during the rest of his life, Muhammad received further revelations from God through Gabriel, which he committed to memory and taught to his friends. Sometimes, floods of rhythmic praise came from his lips. Because Muhammad was uneducated and illiterate, his companions wrote down these words on leaves, stones, bones, and parchment. They became the Quran, the most beautiful and poetic work in the Arabic language. Muslims consider the Quran to be the word of God—eternal, absolute, and irrevocable. *Quran* means "recitation" in Arabic.

In 622, Muhammad left Mecca, where he was persecuted because of his radical new religious philosophy. At that time, Arabs were polytheists (believed in many gods). Yet Islam, like Christianity before it, is a monotheistic religion. Muhammad traveled to Medina, also in Arabia, where he was honored. This year is considered the beginning of the Muslim era and is the first year of the Islamic calendar. From Medina, Islam spread quickly, and by the time Muhammad died in 632, it had reached many thousands of people. It continued to spread rapidly and eventually became the principal religion of the Middle East and of parts of Asia and North Africa. In modern times, Islam is a vital religion and continues to attract people to the faith.

Muslims consider Muhammad the greatest prophet who ever lived, and they acknowledge other prophets such as Abraham, Isaac, Moses, David, and Jesus. Muslims believe that Muhammad is God's last prophet, and therefore, his message is the most complete message to the world.

Islamic Spirituality

Islam has a strong spiritual quality, teaching honesty, generosity, love, and justice. Some people who have studied the religion have converted to it from other religions and find a wonderful sense of peace. They are strong advocates.

The Arabic word *Islam* means "surrender" (to the will of Allah, the all-powerful God who determines the fate of humanity). The word shares its roots with *salaam,* the Arabic word for "peace." Muslims believe that Allah is everywhere. Spiritual life is based on both the love and fear of God, obedience to his will, and a search for the knowledge of God.

SUFISM

One of the most fascinating, colorful, and uplifting spiritual experiences is found in Sufism, a mystical form of Islam followed by both women and men. Sufis reject materialism and follow a spiritual path emphasizing personal harmony with divine love. Sufi orders are centers of spiritual, social, and political life. While traditional Muslims frown upon any use of music in religious rituals, Sufi orders throughout the Islamic world have developed a wide variety of ritual observances involving music.

In the thirteenth century, Sufi mystic and poet Jalal al-Din al-Rumi founded the Mevlani order. Mevlani members, who engage in a musical whirling ceremony, are known as the whirling dervishes. Rumi believed that the natural state of all things is to revolve, and each stage of the dance of the dervishes represents ascent toward union with the divine. By deserting ego and turning toward truth and perfection with loving intent, the dancers are conveying God's spiritual gift and embracing all of humankind with affection and love.

Religious Muslims live a life in which religion and spirituality play a major role. Muslims strive to implement God's will in both their private and public lives. A famous verse from the Quran illustrates how Muslims view their God:

> Allah! There is no God but He, the Living, Who needs no other but Whom all others need. He is never drowsy nor does He rest. Space and the Earth belong to Him; who can intercede without His consent? He knows everything people have done and will do, and no one can grasp the least of His knowledge, without his review. His throne extends over the heavens and the Earth and He doesn't tire in the safekeeping. He alone is the Most High, the Lord Sovereign Supreme.

As part of their prayer practice and in times of personal struggle, many Muslims recite the ninety-nine names of Allah as they handle their prayer beads. The names for God consist of God's qualities, such as the Mighty, the Strong, the Merciful, the Everlasting, the Beginning, the Last, the Avenger of Evil, and the Bringer of Peace. Using prayer beads is believed to purify the heart.

Muslims adhere to the Islamic code during their lifetime and expect to face reckoning after they die. When they die, they believe that the soul lives on in a state of sleep but will be rejoined with the body. The body will return to Earth and the person will be judged by Allah. For this reason, Muslims do not cremate dead bodies. Muslims are promised a paradise after death where there is nearness to God. For those who keep from evil, paradise offers gardens underneath which rivers flow, pure *azwaj* (the perfect mate), and contentment from Allah.

Muslims believe that God resembles nothing else in creation. He has no gender and no form that people can comprehend. Therefore, Islam forbids making pictures or statues of God.

Muslim Life

Islam is a total way of life. Muslims believe in a divine law that guides their daily lives. The Quran dictates what they should wear, eat, and drink. Alcohol is forbidden.

The dress code of Muslims varies from place to place, depending on the country. The Quran instructs men and women to dress modestly. By tradition, many Muslim women wear a hijab, a head scarf, in the presence of men to whom they are not married or related. They wear loose-fitting clothes, and they cover their legs to the ankles and their arms to the wrists. Some cover most of their faces.

A Muslim woman in Germany wears a hijab, a symbol of modesty in the Muslim community.

RELIGION IN AFRICA

While there are local variations, North Africa is pre-dominantly Islamic. Islam is also common in the countries along the east and west coasts of the African continent. In the countries of sub-Saharan Africa to the south of the Sahara—the desert that covers much of North Africa—the majority of people are Christian. In some places, Islam or Christianity is practiced along with a traditional tribal religion, but in many areas, especially rural, tradi-tional African religions dominate. New prophets, who lead their own groups and establish their own churches, are reported in almost all parts of the continent.

Practitioners of many of the traditional religions in Africa believe in a God who creates all things. Numer-ous spirits are thought to exist, such as spirits of the air, earth, sea, lakes and rivers, lightning, and the sun. Indig-enous (local) religions tell stories of tribal origins and early human migrations. Social values are expressed in myths, legends, folktales, and riddles. Magic and sorcery are also part of many traditional, indigenous religions, although in modern times, some of these practices are observed well outside of public view. Most indigenous religions explain how the world was made, how civiliza-tion came about, and what happens after a person dies. Practitioners follow rituals for rites of passage, such as birth, name giving, engagement, marriage, and death. In this way, African religion affirms and celebrates life.

The role of Muslim women and their place in society varies, depending upon how strictly Islam is interpreted and observed. In some Islamic countries, such as Turkey and Malaysia, Muslim women hold high government offices, while in others, such as Saudi Arabia, women have little or no access to the public life of their communities.

Islam is the fastest-growing religion in the world. Muslims are in the majority in fifty-six countries. About 20 percent of Muslims are Arabs. (Not all Arabs are Muslims.) The largest Muslim populations, however, are in Indonesia, Pakistan, Bangladesh, and India.

Serious problems and misunderstandings among religions intensified after the tragedy of September 11, 2001. Terrorists flew airplanes into the World Trade Center in New York City and the Pentagon near Washington, D.C. Al-Qaeda, an international terrorist organization, was responsible for this and many other attacks.

Al-Qaeda is the name of an international Islamist network that consists of radical Muslims advocating, among other things, the imposition of Islamic law, by violent means, if necessary. Yet, the Quran says that whoever takes a life kills all humanity, unless in response to murder or for stopping the spread of disorder on Earth. And whoever saves a life saves all humanity. Although radical Islamists consider their work to be virtuous, most Muslims do not interpret the Quran in the same way and condemn terrorism.

The Baha'i Faith

Hagit is a teen who lives in Saint Lucia, an island in the Caribbean. After school he goes to a Baha'i garden, where he reads books and thinks about his life. He didn't know anything about the Baha'i religion until a friend of his parents invited him to attend Baha'i faith classes at the friend's house. There he asked questions about the religion and was pleased to learn it is a faith based on love and the oneness of humanity. Hagit continues his visits to the garden and says prayers each day.

Unlike Muslims, Baha'is do not believe that Muhammad was the last of the true prophets. Baha'is believe that God sent new information to the world after the time of the great religious leaders—Buddha, Moses, Jesus, and Muhammad. They believe that after the time of these leaders, humankind became more responsible, mature, and ready for a new prophet.

Bahaism originated in the mid-nineteenth century in present-day Iran. It started as a sect (a separate branch) of the Islamic religion. In 1844 a young Muslim, who called himself the Bab (the "gate" of faith, meaning that following him was the way to heaven), advocated sweeping social and religious reforms in Iran. He gathered many followers around him, who were called Babis. Many of his followers were tortured and imprisoned because of their faith, and the government publicly executed the Bab for his faith in 1850. Before he died, the Bab claimed he had prepared the way for a prophet who would come and establish a universal religion.

Mirza Hoseyn Ali Nuri, who came to be known as Baha'u'llah (The Glory of God), was the son of a wealthy family in what is currently Iraq. He was imprisoned by his neighbors because he was a follower of the Bab. In 1863, when he and other Bab disciples were expelled from Baghdad, Iraq, to Constantinople (present-day Istanbul, Turkey), he revealed that he was the promised one of whom the Bab had foretold. Religious scholar J. E. Esslemont explained that Baha'u'llah declared "plainly and repeatedly that he was the long-expected educator and teacher of all peoples, the channel of a wondrous grace that would transcend all previous outpourings, in which all previous forms of religion would become merged, as rivers merge into the ocean."

Although Baha'u'llah was imprisoned, he sent out missionaries (religious teachers) to spread the word of his teachings of unity and world peace. He also wrote many books and letters while he was imprisoned.

His son and grandson continued to spread the religion after his death. They established many groups in many nations. By the time of the grandson's death in 1957, Bahaism was governed by a body of officials from all over the world. The faith is united under the Baha'i World Centre in Israel and is one of the top ten organized religions of the world, with about 7.5 million members.

Baha'is worship daily using a set series of prayers. They pray in the direction of Acre, and Haifa, both in Israel. They are encouraged to pray privately, and they also worship in spiritual assemblies. The following doctrine, which Baha'is believe came directly from God, describes Baha'i teachings: "The Baha'i Faith upholds the unity of God, recognizes the unity of His Prophets, and inculcates [teaches] the principle of oneness and wholeness of the entire human race. It proclaims the necessity of inevitability of the unification of mankind."

NATIVE AMERICAN RELIGIONS

Indigenous religions of North and South America vary widely, but many have connections to the natural world. They are heavily influenced by a history of hunting wild animals and tending to agriculture. Many ceremonies and rituals are also connected with the weather and the sun as well as with plants and animals.

Some indigenous nations believe that the universe was formed in many layers that were linked by a World Tree. The tree had its roots deep in the earth, its trunk passed through their natural world, and its top dwelled in the sky world. Other indigenous peoples of the Americas believe that their ancestors came from beneath the earth, which had many dark layers through which humans had to climb to get to the surface.

The Native American Church, or Peyote Church, is the most widespread indigenous religion among Native Americans. Peyote religion is practiced in fifty Indian nations that include between one hundred thousand to three hundred thousand people. It incorporates both Christianity and tribal religion.

The Apache nation, which inhabits the southwestern part of the United States, is credited with using peyote in religious service. Peyote is a spineless cactus with hallucinogenic effects. It makes users feel closer to God. In many cases, the peyote sacrament is part of a sweat lodge ceremony. A sweat lodge is a structure made of saplings covered with skins, canvas, or blankets. When water is thrown on hot rocks in the sweat lodge, steam is created.

About a dozen men gather in a sweat lodge where they reverently attempt to weave their souls with the rocks and water. Chanting fills the darkness. A chosen individual calls on the Great Powers, gods, to protect those present and the other members of the tribe. The chosen person calls upon the Great Powers to bring strength and power to his people. Then the blanket is lifted from the opening that serves as a door, and the men go outside and roll naked in a body of water, sometimes in the snow, to cleanse their bodies.

Sun dances, spirit dances, and the smoking of peace pipes are also expressions of spirituality among the indigenous peoples of the Americas. Prayers often take place on sacred grounds. As many as eight thousand Native Americans travel to Bear Butte, Montana, each year to spend time praying on the sacred ground there. The Sioux nation calls this location an emergence spot, one where the prophet Sweet Medicine brought the cultural tradition of their people.

When Europeans came to the American continent and encountered indigenous faiths, they viewed spirit worship as inspired by the devil. Through missionaries and their schools, Native Americans were forced to give up their religions and adopt Christianity. In modern times, many American Indians retain some of their original traditions when they worship, while others have become devout Christians. Many combine traditional and Christian spiritualities.

Baha'is believe in creating one world—one government under their faith. They urge the creation of an international language. They strongly emphasize social concerns, praising any work in the spirit of service. They believe in equal rights for men and women and require education for all. They believe that a husband should have only one wife (Islam traditionally allows four wives), and they discourage divorce. Marriage partners may choose each other, but they must

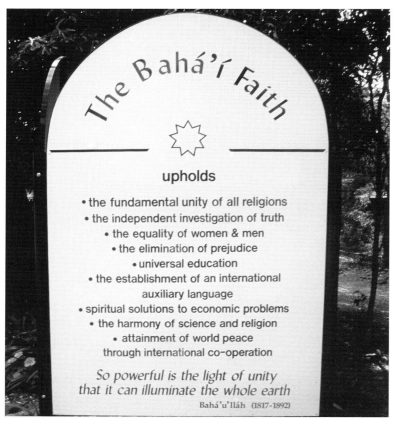

This sign listing the tenets of the Baha'i faith stands in a park in Sydney, Australia.

ask permission of both sets of parents before they marry. Alcohol and other drugs are forbidden, and tobacco use is discouraged. These and other beliefs and teachings are strictly followed.

Most Baha'i communities worship in homes or halls rented or bought for spiritual assemblies. Although only a very small percentage of Iranians and Iraqis are Baha'i, the faith has spread widely, growing in Asia, the Pacific Islands, Africa, and Latin America. Main centers of worship are located in the United States, Germany, India, Uganda, Samoa, and Australia. Religious scholars have described Baha'i as the most widely spread religion after Christianity.

CHAPTER 4

MODERN RELIGIONS

Hundreds of new religions have appeared in modern times. Many modern religions pick up some of their ideas and practices from the occult (a practice of connecting with supernatural or supernormal powers), as well as from traditional organized religions.

Scientology

From Hollywood to Hong Kong, you can see the word *Scientology* on big signs. Many people recognize Scientology only as the religion of some Hollywood celebrities, but it has adherents around the globe.

The Church of Scientology is a religious organization dedicated to the rehabilitation, or healing, of the human spirit. It views humankind as essentially good and with vast potential. Scientology claims to offer step-by-step rehabilitation from life's problems and a way to achieve awareness of a person's spiritual existence. The church provides counseling and rehabilitation programs aimed at achieving these goals and does not support the idea that a god or gods exist.

While some people describe Scientology as a religion, others say it is not a religion at all but a form of behavior therapy. Many critics view it as pseudoscientific, as an unscrupulous commercial organization, or as a cult. The cult status may be because its founder, L. Ron Hubbard (1911–1986), was a pulp-fiction and science-fiction writer. He established the doctrines of Scientology in his book *Dianetics: The Modern Science of Mental Health* (1950).

L. Ron Hubbard (left) *is the founder of Scientology.*

Hubbard claimed that Dianetics can cure physical illness brought on by germs and mental illnesses, which he said are contagious. Scientology and psychiatry have long been at odds about how mental illness should be treated. According to Hubbard, engrams (messages) are stored in the unconscious mind. These engrams make people inefficient, ill, and even insane.

To rid the body of an engram through Dianetics, a person spends time with a counselor (a scientologist who has studied this behavior) on a one-to-one basis. In auditing sessions, the counselor helps the patient achieve a state of reverie—a state of daydreaming—and encourages him or her to recount a painful experience. According to Scientology, these experiences may have occurred before birth. For instance, Scientologists believe that every time a pregnant woman has sexual intercourse, engrams are transmitted to her unborn child. Other experiences that have been stored in the unconscious mind may come forth at these counseling sessions.

Each painful experience is examined and reexperienced in the auditing session so that the engram can be released. A person goes to many auditing sessions to be released from all the engrams that are consciously or unconsciously troubling the person. The person being audited is called a preclear (PC), and a confidential file is kept of all the sessions.

Most auditors (counselors) use an E-meter, a device that measures very small changes in electrical resistance in the body of the preclear. When a preclear holds a can in each hand, a small amount of electricity is passed through the E-meter. A needle on a dial registers changes as the person answers questions from the auditor. Scientologists believe the E-meter helps determine specific areas of concern.

According to Scientology, every person is an immortal human being (a thetan) who has lived through many past lives and will continue to live beyond the death of the body. Auditing helps people advance to higher levels of existence until they reach the state of Operating Thetan (OT), the ultimate goal. The aim of Scientology is to get the soul back to its native state of total freedom, free from all mental and physical ills. This may take hundreds of hours of auditing and can be very expensive. One estimate of Scientology's income from auditing is $300 million a year. Many people drop out of the program because it is too expensive and lengthy. They never reach the state of OT.

The Church of Scientology has a worldwide network of programs dedicated to the promotion of Hubbard's philosophies. They range from drug treatment centers to a consulting firm on Hubbard's management techniques. Scientology has missions around the world, with centers in the United States, Italy, Australia, Japan, New Zealand, and in some cities in South and Central America and Africa. Some of the Celebrity Centres are located in Hollywood (California), New York City (New York), Dallas (Texas), Nashville (Tennessee), Las Vegas (Nevada), London (England), Paris (France), Florence (Italy), and Vienna (Austria).

The true number of people involved in Scientology is unknown. The church claims ten million, while other experts say there are five hundred thousand worldwide. Critics of the church claim the number is much smaller.

Christian Science

Alma is a member of the Church of Christ, Scientist, often called the Christian Science Church. She was born in Germany and was a member of and got married in the Lutheran Church before she came to the United States. Her husband, however, is a Christian Scientist and is very spiritual and faithful to his church. After their marriage, Alma attended meetings with him and decided to accept his religion, even though it was very different from the one she knew when she was growing up.

Christian Scientists believe that the ills of the flesh, meaning any sickness or disease, can be healed by prayer alone. All the same, many Christian Scientists turn to medical care for help. This is especially true when surgery is needed. So when Alma has colds and headaches, she calls in a Christian Science "reader"—a person trained to read certain scriptures. But when she broke her wrist, she went to the hospital to have the bone set.

Alma attends meetings at the local Christian Science Church and has visited the Mother Church, the First Church of Christ, Scientist, in Boston, Massachusetts. She also read the book *Science and Health with Key to the Scriptures* (1875) by Mary Baker Eddy. Mary Baker Eddy founded the Church of Christ, Scientist in 1879. Her spiritual story began when she suffered poor health as a child and in later years. She turned to the Christian Bible for consolation. In February 1866, Mary Baker Eddy slipped on the ice and was injured. Accounts of what happened after the fall differ, but the fall is viewed as the beginning of Christian Science. Eddy taught that healing comes from God,

In 1879, Mary Baker Eddy started the Church of Christ, Scientist, based on her personal experiences.

and it is God's will for us to be well. She wrote *Science and Health with Key to the Scriptures*, which is the authoritative work of the religion. She also founded the newspaper the *Christian Science Monitor.*

Christian Scientists acknowledge one supreme and infinite God and his son, Jesus Christ—the Holy Spirit (a comforter) and a man made in God's image and likeness. Human beings are considered the reflection of a wholly good and perfect God. Christian Science claims to be thoroughly Christian, but not all Christians agree with this.

The widely believed and publicized doctrine of the Christian Scientist Church is: "It is unchristian to believe that pain and sickness are anything but illusions." Christian Science is based on the action of the divine Mind over the human mind and body.

Church of Jesus Christ of Latter-day Saints (Mormons)

Sarah and her parents belong to the Mormon Church. Her classmates used to tease her about not drinking colas, even when she explained that Mormons do not drink alcoholic beverages or sodas with caffeine. They also teased her about having several mothers, even though most Mormons gave up the practice of polygamy—in which one husband has many wives—more than a century ago. Over time, Sarah's classmates realized that she is a great friend, and they no longer tease her. In fact, most of her friends admire her greatly for her contributions to people who are less fortunate.

The Church of Jesus Christ of Latter-day Saints is widely known as the Mormon Church and is headquartered in Salt Lake City, Utah. It is known for its excellent choir, its extensive records of genealogy, and its history of the practice of polygamy, which the church outlawed in 1890. (The United States had made polygamy illegal in 1862.) Mormons are well known for their outstanding work in community service.

American religious leader Joseph Smith (1805–1844) founded the Mormon Church in 1830. At the age of fourteen, Smith became concerned with finding a new Christian spiritual identity. He went into the woods near his home in New York to pray for the truth. There he experienced a vision of God the

*Mormons worship in the Mormon Tabernacle
in Salt Lake City, Utah, at an anniversary event.*

Father and Jesus Christ, and he believed God commanded him to join none of the existing churches. He believed that God called him to be a prophet and to bring back the true church of Christ.

In 1827 Smith said that an angel directed him to a place were he found golden plates with writing on them. The writing was in a language he described as Reformed

Egyptian and, when translated, these writings became the Book of Mormon. They revealed that God evolved from humankind and that men may become gods.

In 1830 Smith and his followers established the Church of Christ in Fayette, New York. This church was intended to be the divine restoration of the Christian Church as it existed in early times. But the Mormons' acceptance of polygamy and other beliefs that did not agree with established Christian practices led to their persecution. As a result, the church moved westward to Ohio, Missouri, and then Nauvoo, Illinois, where local communities also distrusted the Mormons. Violence and legal problems arose out of these tensions, and in 1844, a mob murdered Smith in Carthage, Illinois. His church declared him a martyr, one who suffers rather than give up his religion.

Brigham Young, who had been with the church since 1830, became the church leader after Smith's death. In 1846, when the persecution of the Mormons in Illinois increased, he led them west to land that later became Salt Lake City, Utah.

Mormons gave up polygamy more than a century ago, which led some members to break away from the main church. Known as Fundamentalist Latter-day Saints, these members continue to practice polygamy. Polygamy among Mormans receives media attention in the twenty-first century, especially when minors or abuse are involved. (Not all plural marriages in this religion include minors.)

The membership of the main Church of Jesus Christ of Latter-day Saints continues to grow. In the twenty-first century, it has about five million members worldwide.

Jehovah's Witnesses

Raymond's parents are Jehovah's Witnesses. They are helping to build a new Kingdom Hall, or place of worship, in their hometown. Raymond is studying his religion so that he can be baptized (welcomed into the church through a ritual of purification and initiation). Jehovah's Witnesses do not baptize members until a person has studied Watchtower literature—literature about their religion—and has answered questions before a panel of elders. Raymond hopes he will be ready for baptism before the new Kingdom Hall is finished.

Young people line up to be baptized into the Jehovah's Witnesses faith at a stadium in Prague, Czech Republic.

The Jehovah's Witnesses believe that they are the only people Jesus will redeem at his second coming—his return to Earth. Their founder, Charles Taze Russell, believed that Jesus would return in 1949. When this did not occur, the Jehovah's Witnesses amended their belief to say that Jesus will return soon. They regard themselves as the only true religion and are officially known as the Watchtower Bible and Tract Society.

Jehovah's Witnesses are well known for passing out literature, including the *Watchtower* magazine, door-to-door. The door-to-door visits are an important part of the religion's spiritual practice as a way to convert people to the religion. Jehovah's Witnesses must remain active in distributing literature. As soon as they stop, they are considered dead by peers. To maintain active status, a person must engage in witnessing (evangelizing and Bible study) at least one hour per month, but ten hours is considered the quota for anyone in good standing. Although women help distribute the *Watchtower,* they are considered as "lowly creatures whom God created for man as man's helper."

Jehovah's Witnesses refuse blood transfusions. They cite passages in the Bible that they believe forbid the intake of foreign blood. Even if they are suffering from medical conditions that could be cured by blood transfusions, Jehovah's Witnesses have been known to choose death rather than break faith with their religion.

New Age Spirituality

People of the New Age faith generally believe in monism—a philosophy that says that all that exists is derived from a single source of divine energy. There is no god outside the individual, for the individual is God. What is termed God is within your being. This concept is a central focus of the New Age movement. "We are all gods couched in our own creaturehood" is a common expression among New Age believers. This means keeping the body, mind, and spirit in harmony.

New Age spirituality consists of a wide range of beliefs held by many different individuals. It is not an organized religion. Many followers construct their own religions based on older spiritual traditions, often with elements from Christianity, Native American religions, and Eastern religions. So much variety exists in

ECKHART TOLLE

Eckhart Tolle is a popular author who writes about spirituality and has a large contemporary following. Born in 1948 in Germany, he lives in Vancouver, Canada, and has written best-sellers including *The Power of Now* and *A New Earth: Awakening to Your Life's Purpose*. He is not aligned with any particular religion or tradition, but he reaches many people with his guidance of a way out of suffering and into peace. According to his publishers, he conveys a simple and profound message with the timeless and uncomplicated clarity of ancient spiritual masters.

Television talk-show host Oprah Winfrey has named Tolle's *The Power of Now* as one of her favorite books. And early in 2008, she chose *A New Earth* for the Oprah's Book Club selection and held a free online seminar for those interested in learning more about the subject.

New Age spirituality that one author said it could not be described fully in a thousand pages.

Many aspects of the New Age movement have come from ancient practices. Many New Agers believe in reincarnation and that the quality of the new life will depend on karma.

New Age belief also accepts spiritualism, one of the world's oldest religious beliefs. It is a belief that people are able to communicate with the dead. Picture a medium, a person who contacts spirits of the dead, sitting in a darkened room in a deep trance, along with the mother of two children who have died. The mother has asked the medium to communicate with her children. After a period of silence, the mother hears the voice of her daughter who died seven years ago. The medium talks with her spirit, encouraging her to speak with them. The spirit tells her mother that she is well and that she has her long dead sister with her. The mother is extremely happy and tells her friends of her talk with her daughter.

Channeling is a process within the New Age movement in which individuals claim to empty themselves of their own consciousness and invite spirits of the dead to temporarily assume control of their body. The spirit speaks through the channeler. Other New Age beliefs include astrology as a method of foretelling the future, tarot cards—cards used for fortune-telling—as a reliable basis for making decisions, and crystals as a source of energizing power or healing.

Indigo children are named for the deep blue aura that these children are said to radiate. According to New Agers, auras are fields of subtle, multicolored luminous light that surrounds living bodies. Indigo

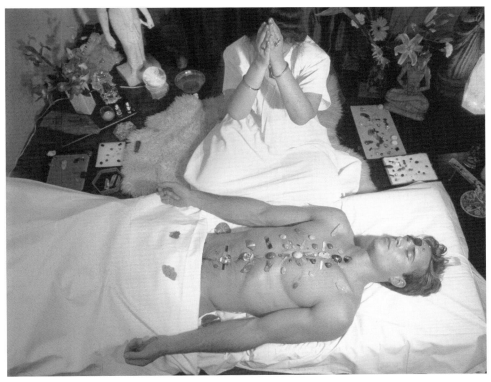

Belief in the power of crystals and meditation
is part of the New Age movement.

children are the hope of many New Agers because
they believe that Indigos have come to Earth to create a new World of Peace. According to the New Age
movement, Earth has left the astrological Age of
Pisces, which began about the time of the birth of
Christ. Two thousand years later, we have entered a
new astrological age, known as the Age of Aquarius,
which, according to these believers, is a golden age
that promises a glorious future.

CHAPTER 5

THE SPIRIT AFTER
THE BODY DIES

What happens after the body dies? A wide
variety of religions and spiritual practices ponder this
question, and in fact, reports of near-death experiences are common. For example, one minister can
describe how he died in an accident, went to heaven
for ninety minutes, and came back to Earth. He
described heaven, with its gate at which long dead
relatives and friends greeted him.

Many others have described this experience too.
Here is a somewhat typical description from a person
with a near-death experience:

I hovered over my body that was lying on the bed.
It was the first time I had seen it in three dimensions
since a mirror only shows it in two. I felt peaceful,

even though I recognized that my body was lifeless. Then I felt a surge of energy, and I was completely free of pain even though a large tumor had just been surgically removed from my stomach. I felt that I had been reborn into a life of peace, love, and joy.

I could move forward freely without moving my arms or legs. I knew that my family would miss me, but I could not feel sorrow. Darkness was all around me, and I was drawn up into a tunnel. I felt myself traveling rapidly through it toward the light at the end. I seemed to be moving quickly. As I drew closer to it, the light became brighter than the sun. I was floating toward beautiful colors and listening to glorious singing. Then I found myself in my hospital room again, and I knew that I had not really died. I just had a wonderful taste of what heaven was like.

This is just one example of a near-death experience. Many people describe different experiences, but they all have much in common. They are always different from dreams and hallucinations, and they are not a sign of mental illness.

Many people who have had near-death experiences mention feeling very peaceful and seeing a tunnel with a light at the end. Some report reviewing their life experiences. Many people meet others, some who have died earlier, and see symbols from their own or other religions. They also tell of a boundary—such as a fence, a cliff, or water—that may not be crossed if they are to return to life. Many felt that they had to return to life to help loved ones who need them. Just about all report an out-of-body sensation.

A near-death experience can have strong effects on a person. About 80 percent of the people who have reported these experiences claim that their lives were forever changed by what happened to them. Most of them had a renewed zest for life and a more spiritual outlook. Some people are relieved, some are angry, and many are disoriented. Some people feel that they have a greater sensitivity, more compassion for others, and a heightened sense of purpose.

Although the person who has a near-death experience often believes he or she is the only one who has felt this way, this kind of experience is not rare. Near-death experiences have been reported from many cultures around the world. About 13 million adults in the United States alone have reported near-death experiences, and many children experience them too.

Medical and psychological explanations of near-death experiences help show what happens, but they do not explain the whole picture. Scientists believe that the people are experiencing something in the temporal lobes, the lobes at the sides of the brain that are important in hearing, emotions, the sense of identity, and personal integration.

The experience of going through a dark tunnel may be explained by the cutoff of blood and oxygen to these lobes, but it cannot explain the brilliant light and blissful emotions that many people describe. These may be due to different chemicals in the brain near the time of death, but if that is the case, everyone should have the same type of near-death experience. Yet, about 10 percent of these experiences are reported as negative and the rest as blissful.

The International Association for Near-Death Studies, known as IANDS, was founded in Connecticut in 1978. It includes health-care workers, researchers,

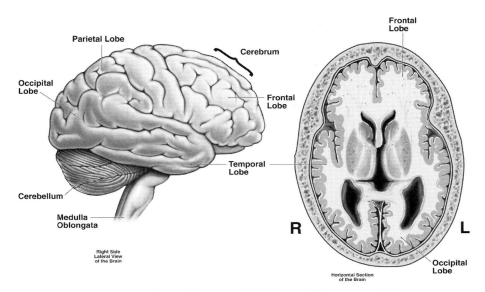

This illustration shows the parts of the brain. The temporal lobes are the lower sides of the brain. Some scientists have linked near-death experiences to this part of the brain.

scientists, and a variety of other people who are interested in learning more about near-death experiences. The association publishes two quarterly periodicals and other informational materials. Also, many support groups exist for those who need emotional support and for those who want to learn more about other people who have had near-death experiences.

What Is Soul?

The religions practiced around the world are various, but many of them are concerned with the soul. You may talk about *Body + Soul* as the name of a magazine, or about soul food, such as collard greens, yams, corn bread, and rice. Or you may say you are trying to find your soul mate. Jazz musicians are often described as having soul, and a grandmother or kindly neighbor might be a nice old soul.

You might describe someone as being the soul of discretion, one who could be trusted not to tell your secrets. You might talk about someone as a lost soul, one that has trouble coping with life. You may read about a character who is selling his soul to the devil. Or you may know someone who devotes his or her life to saving souls. But what is soul?

Many people believe the soul is the spiritual or immaterial part of a human being as compared with the physical body. It is the living, dynamic part of each individual. According to Deepak Chopra, famous author of books on spirituality, soul exists as

Deepak Chopra has made a career out of helping people gain deeper awareness of their souls and to develop mind-body-spirit wellness.

consciousness, or awareness, and therefore must be found in consciousness. Chopra says the soul grows and deepens the more you devote yourself to it.

According to Michael Shermer, publisher of *Skeptic* magazine, the human essence is more than a pile of parts. He believes that the soul is a unique pattern that represents a person. So, even if scientists could build a physical body, it would lack the soul that makes it human.

In some religions, the soul is regarded as immortal—it never dies. It leaves the body at death and lives apart from the body. According to Sikhism, Buddhism, and Hinduism, the soul lives after the death of the body and is reborn in another body. This reincarnation continues until a person finally achieves a state of spiritual perfection.

In Islam a person's soul is the original spirit that Allah breathed into Adam. It is endowed with good and evil. The souls of the dead stay near Allah, and on the Day of Judgment, they will be reunited with their risen bodies.

Finding the Soul

Many people believe that the soul leaves the body at the time of death, but no one has ever been able to scientifically locate where it is before it leaves. Some people believe that the soul is located in the temporal lobes of the brain, but no one has ever proved this.

A number of researchers have performed experiments investigating the existence of the soul by comparing the weight of the brain before death and the weight of the same brain immediately after death, when they believe the soul has left. Author Mary Roach, in her book *Spook* (2005), describes in detail some scientists who weighed a variety of animals just after they died to compare their weight with the weight before they died. She tells of an experiment in which a man even set up a soul-weighing operation in his barn.

Duncan MacDougall was in medical school in 1893 when he weighed people in an effort to learn the weight of their souls. He arranged to have consumptives (people with tuberculosis) die while they were lying on a large scale. He carefully weighed them at the time of death and compared that weight with that just after death. In one case, he found the difference of three-quarters of an ounce (21 grams). (A movie exploring the interconnection of life, love, and death, *21 Grams*, was released in 2003.) MacDougall was unable to confirm this with further experiments. Scientists believe that MacDougall's experiments were flawed because of the methods he used and because the sample was too small for a truly acceptable scientific experiment.

Although scientists tried experiments with rats, even sealing them in test tubes, and with dogs, scientists never found the weight of the soul. Even after many experiments, they could not answer the question, Do animals have souls?

Ghosts

Do you believe in ghosts? About 32 percent of people in the United States say they do. Ghosts are apparitions, the spirits or souls, of dead people. Ghosts are often thought to resemble people, appearing in the clothing they wore and in an area they frequented. They may also appear as misty figures in glass windows or in the air.

Ghosts may haunt castles, bedrooms, prisons, cemeteries, churches, and just about any place. Some people will not buy or live in a house that has belonged to someone who committed suicide because they believe that the person's spirit is still there. Many people may be familiar with the "spirits" who set rocking chairs in motion. Ghost hunting, or searching for ghosts in dark places, is popular fun. Some serious ghost hunters spend hundreds of dollars on equipment, such as electromagnetic meters, to find areas where ghosts might be.

Ghosts and spirits have been reported in all parts of the world and in all cultures. People have reported seeing a ghost in a place where another person has seen it before, even though the second person had no knowledge of the first appearance. Many spirit and ghost sightings can be explained as hallucinations, but many cannot be explained. In the 1880s, scientists felt that science would explain in the next twenty-five years whether or not the dead could speak to the living. But that time passed, and many people are still seeking the answer.

Heaven and Hell

Ghosts or no ghosts, the idea of the soul going to heaven or hell after death is widespread. Not everyone agrees when the soul will arrive, and little has been suggested about how it gets there, but descriptions of heaven and hell abound.

In Christianity, heaven is the spiritual state or place where one is with God and has eternal happiness. Most Christians regard the soul as the immortal essence of a person. People will be judged after death by God, who knows all the right and wrong they did during their lives. If they have repented their sins, put their trust in Jesus Christ, and led a good life, they will inherit eternal life in the kingdom of heaven. Otherwise, they may go to hell, a place of eternal punishment.

Individual Christians have various ideas about heaven. If Christian children are asked to draw a picture of heaven, many will draw angels playing harps. The idea that heaven is a physical place has existed since the dawn of human civilization. Some people think it is a physical place above the clouds where God and angels are watching over human beings and that the stars are lights shining from heaven.

In the modern age of science and spaceflight, the idea of heaven as a place in the universe has been abandoned by many, including Christians. Pope John Paul II (1920–2005) said that heaven "is neither an abstraction nor a physical place in the clouds, but a living, personal relationship with the Holy Trinity." However, many Christians still believe they will meet their relatives and friends in heaven.

Judaism does not teach a belief in heaven as a future place for good souls but as a place where God resides. Some scholars believe that an afterlife for Jews developed late in Jewish history. Some Jews believe they may be reunited with loved ones, while sinners are excluded from this reunion. Many Jews believe life ends at death.

A variety of religions have described heaven in specific detail. For example, in Islam, the Quran describes heaven vividly and explicitly as a place of joy where there are fountains of wine and beautiful gardens. A glorious future beyond imagination awaits the believer after death. In Islam (and Christianity), some people follow religious laws for the sake of paradise after death.

Baha'is believe that the soul begins in the ninth month in the mother's womb. While in the womb, the spiritual and intellectual tools necessary for life in the next world are acquired. While one cannot control life in the womb, spiritual and intellectual development after birth depends on individual effort.

In Jainism all human beings have the potential to become gods by conquering worldly passions such as desire, hatred, anger, greed, and pride in one's own personal affairs. People who rid themselves of karma attain peace and contentment. They reach the final destination of eternal bliss, ending all cycles of birth and death.

When Hindus die, the entry into heaven or hell is decided by the Lord of Death, who looks over the accounts of good and bad deeds during a person's lifetime. Heaven is only temporary and lasts until the next birth. Each soul rises through lower life-forms to higher ones before achieving human form. Many reincarnations may occur before the point of release from the recurrent lives and deaths. Hindus hope to achieve moksha. In this permanent state after death, the soul is liberated from the cycles of birth and death when the person becomes one with the divine.

Buddhists also believe that they pass through many births and deaths before the final release into nirvana.

This state of spiritual liberation means being free from passions such as lust, anger, and craving. It is a state of great inner peace and contentment. Buddha discouraged speculation into the state of enlightenment after death, saying that such speculation is not useful in pursuing enlightenment.

Some students have spent much time trying to learn more about what happens when a person dies and have studied reports of near-death experiences. Many people have simply concluded that life after death may exist, but it cannot ever be known by living humans.

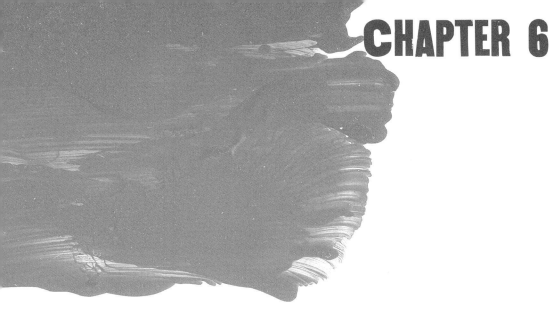

CHAPTER 6

ARE YOU HARDWIRED FOR GOD?

Several twenty-first century books claim that religion is superstition that will fade away as people evolve. However, many experiments seem to indicate that people may be hardwired for God. As modern scientists are beginning to look at a neural basis, one based on nerve cells, for religion, they find that spiritual experiences are biologically and observably real.

People of every culture and land have common spiritual experiences. In a 2007 Harris Poll in the United States, 82 percent of people said they believed in God. Only 6 percent were atheists, who do not believe in a higher being or divine spirit. However, atheists do believe in human goodness and many are spiritual without believing in God.

Some hardwired instincts have long been known. The fear of snakes is a hardwired fear so great that many people get upset just talking about them. The fear of heights is inborn. Babies who have never fallen from a height crawl away from the edge of a cliff. Some modern scientists think that belief in God is as natural as our instincts to flee or fight.

Neurotheology

Birds build the kinds of nests their parents built. Bees build hives with a hexagonal pattern. A place in their brains determines this behavior—they are hardwired to do it.

Areas in the human brain dictate hearing, vision, and the multitude of other functions of the body. A place for reasoning and places for memory and image-making all exist. Could there be a place in the brain linked to spiritual thoughts? Could there be a place that causes humans to search for spiritual experiences? Could there be a "God spot"?

These are questions that scientists have been exploring in a field known as neurotheology. This is the study of the neurobiology of the nerves, or neurons, in the brain and theology, or the study of religion. Neurotheologists are trying to learn more about where spiritual thoughts take place and more about what it means to be human.

Dr. Herbert Benson, known for his book *The Relaxation Response* (1992), states that his scientific studies conclusively show that our bodies are wired to believe and that our bodies are nourished and healed by prayer and other exercises of belief. His studies have shown that brains change with meditation, from beginners to people who spend their lives practicing it.

Neural Basis for Religious Experience

In 1997 Vilayanur Ramachandran of the University of California in San Diego told the Society of Neuroscience that there is a neural basis for spiritual experiences. He believed that enhancements in the electrical activity of the temporal lobes are responsible for spiritual experience. This part of the brain, known as the emotional brain, has a connection with very strong religious feelings for a minority of patients who suffer from temporal lobe epilepsy.

One man, an atheist who had temporal lobe epilepsy, had a powerful religious vision that made him feel he had gone to hell. He was very frightened by the idea that he might stay there because he had not been a devout Christian. A woman, who suffered from the same disease, believed that her newborn baby was Jesus and that she was Mary, his mother, and her husband was Joseph. She expressed pleasure at being part of the holy family.

Ramachandran set up experiments to compare the brains of people with and without temporal lobe epilepsy. Using equipment that showed responses in skin resistance, he could tell how much they sweated when looking at different kinds of imagery. People with the disease responded dramatically to religious words and symbols, much more than religious people without epilepsy did. This and later experiments indicated that the temporal lobes are a key in experiencing spirituality. Some scientists believe that what happens in the minds of these people with temporal lobe epilepsy are extreme cases of what goes on in the minds of everyone.

To learn more about religion and the brain, Michael Persinger of Laurentian University in Canada has experimented with volunteers who wear what is commonly called a God Helmet. This is a headpiece, somewhat like a motorcycle helmet, rigged with electromagnets that produce a weak magnetic field, one that is no stronger than that from a computer monitor. The magnetic field triggers bursts of electricity in the temporal lobes just like during temporal lobe epilepsy seizures.

As a result of his experiments, Persinger found that when the left region of the brain is stimulated and

A woman undergoes testing in a helmet designed to induce religious experiences. The helmet was created by Michael Persinger and Stanley Koren.

the right is not, the left interprets the stimulation as a presence, often that of God. About 80 percent of the subjects in these experiments experience a presence in the room or a oneness with the universe.

Some religious people reject the idea of a God spot in the human brain. They feel that such experiments are a challenge to religion. Other people feel that these studies support the existence of God.

Dr. Dean Hamer, head of Gene Structure and Regulation at the National Cancer Institute, searched for a God gene, or a section of DNA (genetic material) that includes the tendency to pray often and to feel the presence of God. Hamer points out that belief in God could involve hundreds of genes, but people with what he believes to be the God gene seemed likelier to feel that they could go beyond the range of human experience and feel more spiritual. He wrote a book called *The God Gene: How Faith Is Hardwired into Our Genes* (2004). According to Hamer's book, there seems to be a gene for belief in God. His book created a great deal of discussion about the underpinnings of spirituality.

Hamer agreed that his findings did not speak of the reality of the existence of God. His findings, he said, are agnostic (a belief that God may exist but cannot be known by humans). Some readers claim that there is no more religious significance in his finding than there is to any advancement in the understanding of biology.

Why God Won't Go Away

Dr. Andrew Newberg takes another approach to how spirituality plays out in the brain. He and Dr. Eugene D'Aquili, both of the University of Pennsylvania, have done years of work in the field of neurotheology. They and freelance writer Vince Rause describe some of this work in the book *Why God Won't Go Away: Brain Science and the Biology of Belief* (2002). They hope to encourage laypersons (nonspecialists) to explore their feelings about religion and science and deepen their understanding of both. Their experiments help in bridging the gap in the understanding of world religions.

One of the exciting aspects of the work of Newberg and D'Aquili is the discovery that the sense of self in worshippers gradually changes as they approach deep spiritual states. Consider a volunteer, who is skilled in the practice of meditation, sitting on the floor in a room lit only by a candle. He has some twine next to him that extends under a door to the outside of the room. Scientists are waiting outside the door for a signal, a tug on the twine that will come when the man reaches the highest point, a peak, in his meditation.

When the signal comes, the scientists will inject a radioactive tracer into the intravenous line in the volunteer's arm. Then they will whisk the man away to a machine that can detect the tracer and measure the blood flow in his brain. This helps determine the activity of the neurons in the brain. Brain changes are imaged on a computer.

The scientists find that an area toward the top and back of the brain appears dark. This area determines where the body ends and the rest of the world begins. They call it the orientation area. During meditation, this area is blocked from sensory input. This prevents the brain from understanding the difference between self and nonself. Scientists believe this wiping away of the sense of self is connected to feelings of peace and an awareness of God's presence.

Newberg and D'Aquili suggest that the brain does not invent this supreme religious state but instead finds it. They speculate that all world religions may trace their origins back through culturally diverse interpretations of this same mental state.

In addition to being produced by stimulation of the temporal lobes and other parts of the brain, spiritual feelings can be produced by some drugs. For many years, the Aztecs—indigenous people of Mexico before the Spanish conquest in the 1500s—used psilocybin, the active component in a species of mushrooms that produces hallucinations, in their religious ceremonies. In 2006 Dr. Roland Griffiths and his colleagues at Johns Hopkins University in Maryland did controlled experiments with psilocybin on religious volunteers. Ritalin, a drug that calms hyperactive children but stimulates others, was used as a placebo (a harmless substance given as if it were medicine).

About 20 percent of the participants in the experiment described their experience as dominated by anxiety. But more than one-third of the volunteers who received psilocybin said that they had the most spiritually significant experience of their lifetimes. Dr. Solomon Snyder, a colleague of Dr. Griffiths, said that investigations of psilocybin and similar drugs could help scientists understand the molecular changes in the brain that underlie spiritual experience.

Scientists are just beginning to learn what takes place physically during spiritual experiences. *Why God Won't Go Away* ends with the powerful statement: "As long as our brains are arranged the way they are, as long as our minds are capable of sensing this deeper reality, spirituality will continue to shape the human experience, and God, however we define that majestic, mysterious concept, will not go away." It seems possible that people have always been and will always be spiritual beings.

GLOSSARY

agnostic: a person who believes that it is impossible for humans to know if God exists or not

Allah: the Arabic word for "God"

ascension: the Christian belief that Christ rose into heaven after his resurrection

asceticism: a way of spiritual life that involves self-denial

atheist: one who does not believe in a god or gods

atonement: the belief within Abrahamic religions of the reconciliation of God and humankind

bar mitzvah/bat mitzvah: a celebration for a Jewish boy or girl, on the occasion of the thirteenth birthday, at which the child is welcomed as an adult member of the Jewish community

Bible: the holy book of Jews and Christians

born again: within the Christian tradition, to experience a renewed or confirmed commitment of faith, especially after an intense religious experience

Brahma: a Hindu god who is the creator of the universe

Brahman: the Hindu concept of a universal soul; the priestly caste within Hindu society

Buddhism: a religion based on the teachings of Buddha, who explains the nature of suffering and how to avoid it

caste: the hierarchical social classes of traditional Hindu society. Caste was outlawed in India in 1950.

channeling: in New Age faiths, a process in which a person transmits and receives messages from the dead

Christianity: a religion that proclaims Jesus as the son of God and savior who died for the sins of the world

Confucianism: a system of morality taught by Confucius, a Chinese philosopher

disciple: a follower; also one of the original followers of Jesus Christ

ecospirituality: the awakening of self through the wonders of nature; a spiritual view of people's relationship with the universe

engrams: in Scientology, records of perceptions stored in the brain. Some of these experiences may have occurred prior to birth.

enlightenment: in Buddhism the state of being aware of the true nature of existence

Evangelical Christianity: a form of Christianity that emphasizes being born again, that interprets the Bible literally, and that engages in spreading the word of God to gain converts

Four Noble Truths: the four foundation principles of Buddhism—suffering exists, desire is the reason for suffering, ending suffering is possible, and the way to end suffering is through the Noble Eightfold Path

hajj: the pilgrimage to Mecca—an Islamic holy city in modern Saudi Arabia. According to Islam's Five Pillars of Faith, Muslims must try to make the pilgrimage at least once during their lifetime, if possible.

hijab: a head scarf some Muslim women wear as a display of modesty

Hinduism: one of the world's oldest religions, which has many sets of beliefs that are represented in numerous traditions. Almost all Hindus believe that the real self (atman) is distinct from the temporary body made of matter.

immortal: to live forever; not subject to death

Islam: the religion of Muslims, based on the teachings of Muhammad, which include belief in one god, prayer, fasting, charity, and pilgrimage, as taught in the Quran

Jainism: an Indian religion with doctrines similar to Buddhism

Jehovah's Witness: a religion believing that the end of the world is near. Door-to-door visits are an important part of the religion's spiritual practice as a way to convert people to the religion.

Judaism: the religion of the Jewish people, who believe in one God and the teachings of the Torah—the first five books of the Hebrew Bible—and the Talmud

Kaaba: a small stone building in the court of the Great Mosque at Mecca, Saudi Arabia, that contains a sacred black stone. The Kaaba is the goal of the Islamic pilgrimage to Mecca and is the point toward which Muslims turn during daily prayers.

kami: in the Shinto tradition, the spirits that inhabit the natural world

karma: according to Hinduism and Buddhism, the sum of the quality of acts in this and past lives

kirpan: a small dagger carried by male Sikhs

martyr: one who suffers or dies rather than give up religious faith

materialism: excessive concern about physical possessions

mezuzah: in Jewish houses, the tiny scrolls in small boxes that are affixed to doorposts

moksha: in Hindu belief, the release from the cycle of death and rebirth; eternal spiritual bliss

monism: a common New Age belief that all beings arise from a unified substance; all is one

monotheism: religions that support the belief in one god

Mormonism: a religion founded in the United States in 1830; also called the Church of Jesus Christ of Latter-day Saints

muezzin: the person who calls the Muslim community to prayer five times a day

mythology: a group of ideas and stories that express truths not based on scientific fact

neurotheology: the scientific study of the neurobiology of religion and spirituality

New Age movement: a collection of beliefs in various techniques to develop altered consciousness as a way to express human divinity. New Age thinking accepts no reality outside what a person is able to determine on an experiential basis.

nirvana: within Hinduism and Buddhism, a state of complete release from suffering

Noble Eightfold Path: the ideal life path as expressed in Buddhist thinking; a path that leads to the release of the human desires and passions that cause suffering

Operating Thetan: the stage in Scientology when self-imposed limitations have been relinquished

117

Orthodox Jews: those who strictly observe the ritual laws of Judaism. Hassidic Jews are the strictest of the Orthodox Jews.

parable: a story that illustrates a moral or religious principle

Passover: an eight-day celebration to commemorate the time when Jews were delivered from slavery in ancient Egypt. Passover is celebrated in the spring.

prophet: a person who acts as a divine messenger; a spiritual spokesperson

qigong: in Taoist practice, a series of exercises and movements to reduce stress

Quran: the holy book of Islam. Muslims believe that the Quran contains the complete expression of God's actual words, as dictated by the prophet Muhammad in Arabic.

Ramadan: a month in the Islamic calendar of reflection and fasting every day from dawn to sunset. Because Islamic holidays follow a lunar (moon) calendar, this month falls in different seasons over time.

reincarnation: a central belief in Hinduism and Buddhism of being born into a different body after death

resurrection: rising from the dead; in Christianity, Jesus' rising and life after death

Rosh Hashanah: the Jewish New Year, which falls in autumn

Salat: the daily prayer ritual of Muslims

Scientology: a belief system based on L. Ron Hubbard's book *Dianetics: The Modern Science of Mental Health*

shaman: a person who consults the spiritual world to help or heal another being

Shintoism: the native religion of Japan, which involves the worship of ancestors and the spirits of nature

Shiva: a Hindu god, who is both the destroyer of the universe and its re-creator

Sikhism: an Indian religion that blends certain elements of Hinduism and Islam

soul: the nonmaterial, animating, and spiritual essence of being

spiritualism: a belief in communicating with the dead

tai chi: a Taoist spiritual practice of exercise and movement

Talmud: a collection of Jewish religious law, consisting of two documents known as the Mishnah and the Gemara

Taoism: one of the main religions of China, along with Confucianism and Buddhism, that was founded in the first century B.C.

thetan: in Scientology, an immortal spirit with limitless powers. Every human being is one, according to Scientology.

Torah: the first five books of the Hebrew Bible; the central sacred books of Judaism

torii: a gateway to a Japanese Shinto shrine

Veda: ancient Hindu scriptures

Vishnu: a Hindu god; the preserver of the universe

yarmulke: a small head covering worn by a Jewish man to show respect for God

yin and yang: a circular symbol that represents the balance of the universe in Taoism

Yom Kippur: in the Jewish religion, the day of atonement, which falls in the autumn

SOURCE NOTES

10 William James, *The Varieties of Religious Experience* (New York: Longman, 1902), 53.

20 *Bhagavad Gita For Everyone In All The Worlds,* n.d., http://www. bhagavad-gita.org/ (May 21, 2008).

44 John R. Hinnells, ed., *New Penguin Handbook of Living Religions* (New York: Penguin Books, 2003), 314.

47 Ibid., 320.

52 Proverbs 16:32 (Revised Standard Version).

58 Luke 10:25–29 (RSV).

59 Luke 10:36–37 (RSV).

60 Matthew 21:8 (RSV).

61 John 3:16 (RSV).

69 Quran 96:1-5, quoted in A. J. Arberry, trans., *The Quran Interpreted* (New York: Macmillan, 1955), 344.

72 Quran 2:255.

77 Ruth A. Tucker, *Another Gospel: Cults, Alternative Religion and the New Age Movement* (Grand Rapids, MI: Zondervan, 1989), 286.

77 Elizabeth, Breuilly, Joanne O'Brien., and Martin Palmer, *Religions of the World: The Illustrated Guide to Origins, Beliefs, Traditions and Festivals* (New York: Facts on File, 2005), 152.

87–88 Tucker, 171.

92 Ibid., 138.

104 John Paul II, "Heaven, Hell and Purgatory," July 21, 1999, http://www.etwtn.com/library/PAPALDOC/JP2HEAVN.HTM (May 21, 2008).

113–114 Andrew Newberg, Eugene D'Aquili, and Vince Rause, *Why God Won't Go Away: Brain Science and the Biology of Belief* (New York: Ballantine, 2001), 172.

SELECTED BIBLIOGRAPHY

Albright, Madeleine. *The Mighty and the Almighty: Reflections on America, God and World Affairs.* New York: Harper-Collins, 2006.

Breully, Elizabeth, Joanne O'Brien, and Martin Palmer. *Religions of the World: The Illustrated Guide to Origins, Beliefs, Traditions and Festivals.* New York: Facts on File, 2005.

Collins, Francis S. *The Language of God: A Scientist Presents Evidence for Belief.* New York: Free Press, 2006.

Feldman, Noah. *Divided by God.* New York: Farrar, Straus and Giroux, 2005.

Hallman, J. C. *The Devil Is a Gentleman: Exploring America's Religious Fringe.* New York: Random House, 2006.

Harris, Sam. *The End of Faith: Religion, Terror and the Future of Reason.* New York: W. W. Norton, 2005.

Hay, David. *Something There: The Biology of the Human Spirit.* West Conshohocken, PA: Templeton Foundation Press, 2007.

Heela, Paul, and Linda Woodhead. *The Spiritual Revolution: Why Religion Is Giving Way to Spirituality.* Malden, MA: Blackwell Publishing Company, 2005.

Hinnells, John R. *The New Penguin Handbook of Living Religions*. New York: Penguin Books, 2003.

Hopfe, Lewis M., and Mark R. Woodward. *Religions of the World*. Upper Saddle River, NJ: Pearson, 2005.

James, William. *The Varieties of Religious Experience*. New York: Longman, 1902.

Schmidt, Leigh Eric. *Restless Souls: The Making of American Spirituality from Emerson to Oprah*. New York: HarperCollins, 2005.

Smith, Huston. *The World's Religions: Our Great Wisdom Traditions*. New York: HarperOne, 1991.

Steiger, Brad. *Real Ghosts, Restless Spirits, and Haunted Places*. Canton, MI: Visible Ink Press, 2003.

Tolle, Eckhart. *A New Earth: Awakening to Your Life's Purpose*. New York: Dutton, 2005.

Tucker, Ruth A. *Another Gospel: Cults, Alternative Religion and the New Age Movement*. Grand Rapids, MI: Zondervan, 1989.

FOR FURTHER INFORMATION

Books

Lugira, Aloysius M. *African Religions*. New York: Facts on File, 2004.

Mann, Gurinder Singh. *Buddhists, Hindus, and Sikhs in America*. New York: Oxford University Press, 2002.

Metcalf, Franz. *Buddha in Your Backpack*. Berkeley, CA: Seastone, 2003.

Newberg, Andrew, Eugene D'Aquili, and Vince Rause. *Why God Won't Go Away: Brain Science and the Biology of Self*. New York: Ballantine Books, 2001.

Roach, Mary. *Spook: Science Tackles the Afterlife*. New York: W. W. Norton, 2005.

Sandler, Lauren. *Righteous: Dispatches from the Evangelical Youth Movement*. New York: Viking, 2006.

Smith, Christian. *Soul Searching: The Religious and Spiritual Life of Teenagers*. New York: Oxford, 2005.

Winston, Diana. *Wide Awake: A Buddhist Guide for Teens*. New York: Tandem Library, 2003.

Websites

African Traditional Religion

> http://www.afrikaworld.net/afrel/
> This site provides information on traditional African beliefs and the three main religions of Africa.

The Baha'is

> http://www.baha'i.org
> This is the international website of the Baha'i faith. It provides information on the basics of Bahaism.

Buddhism

> http://www.buddhanet.net/
> This website includes a wide range of information on Buddhism.

Christianity

> http://www.bbc.co.uk/religion/religions/christianity/
> This website provides an introduction to information on Christianity.

Confucianism and Confucian Studies

> http://www.confucianstudies.com/
> This is an online resource for scholars and students of Confucianism, religion of China, and Chinese thought.

Heaven and Hell

> http://plato.stanford.edu/entries/heaven-hell/
> This website offers descriptions of heaven and hell from the perspective of various religions.

International Association for Near-Death Studies

> http://www.iands.org/
> This website provides information about near-death experiences.

Islam

> http://www.islam101.com/
> This is an educational site on the religion of Islam as well as Islamic civilization and culture.

Jainism

> http://www.Jainism.com

This site provides resources, information, and essays on the beliefs of Jainism.

Judaism 101

http://www.jewfaq.org/index.htm

This is an online encyclopedia of Judaism covering Jewish beliefs, people, places, things, language, scripture, holidays, practices, and customs.

The Kabbalah Centre

http://www.kabbalah.com

This website provides comprehensive information on modern Kabbalah, with teaching tools, classes, videos, books, blogs, and where to find more information.

Native American Spiritualities

http://www.religioustolerance.org/nataspir.htm

This website provides an introduction as well as quotations and summaries of the beliefs of various Native American groups.

Religion Facts

http://www.religionfacts.com/

This website strives to be an objective guide to the world's religions. It provides a wealth of information on what religion is and includes details on many different religions and spiritualities.

Religious Tolerance

http://www.religioustolerance.org

This website promotes religious tolerance, freedom, and understanding by describing controversial topics from all viewpoints.

Shintoism

http://www.dishq.org/religions/shintoism.htm

This website includes information on Shinto theology and sayings.

The Sikhism Homepage

http://www.sikhs.org/topics.htm

This website provides information about Sikhism, including its origins and its philosophies and scriptures.

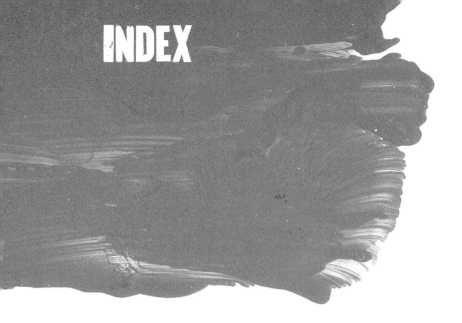

INDEX